HIDDEN TREASURES

DEVON

Edited by Simon Harwin

First published in Great Britain in 2002 by
YOUNG WRITERS
Remus House,
Coltsfoot Drive,
Peterborough, PE2 9JX
Telephone (01733) 890066

HB ISBN 0 75433 770 7
SB ISBN 0 75433 771 5

Foreword

This year, the Young Writers' Hidden Treasures competition proudly presents a showcase of the best poetic talent from over 72,000 up-and-coming writers nationwide.

Young Writers was established in 1991 and we are still successful, even in today's technologically-led world, in promoting and encouraging the reading and writing of poetry.

The thought, effort, imagination and hard work put into each poem impressed us all, and once again, the task of selecting poems was a difficult one, but nevertheless, an enjoyable experience.

We hope you are as pleased as we are with the final selection and that you and your family continue to be entertained with *Hidden Treasures Devon* for many years to come.

Contents

The Poems

THE SUN

I am big,
I am orange,
I'm a round fireball
And I live in the sky
Where it's lovely and cool.

I waken up the flowers,
I put the moon to sleep,
I have the power of shadows,
From my head to feet.

I can make people boil,
I can make people sweat,
I awake in the morning
And at night I set.

For I am the . . .

Abigail Harrison (10)
All Saints CE Primary School

GRAVEYARD

Stone yard,
All bared.

Ghost place,
White face.

Gravestones,
Skeleton bones.

Dark night,
Dog's bite.

Graveyard.

Jessica Williams (11)
All Saints CE Primary School

DRAGON

Fire I can breathe to burn my prey,
You have been warned, stay out of my way.

I can fly like a bird and hover like a bee,
I can soar through the sky over land and sea.

Any animal I can kill,
Spreading the gory blood on the hill.

Water shall put out my flame
And it will leave me with an embarrassing pain.

See me fly, hear me roar,
I can kill a dinosaur.

For I am a dragon.

Daniel Evans (11)
All Saints CE Primary School

THE WEB-FOOTED GECKO

Slimy like a UFO,
Fast, flimsy food for the hyena,
Its big black beady eyes,
Its large webbed feet,
Help it to survive,
Translucent skin,
Its teeth remind me of tiny gemstones.

Natalie Heed (11)
All Saints CE Primary School

TORNADO

I shall break anything in my path,
When I do it I shall laugh.

I can rip off a house top,
Nothing will make me stop.

I make a whistling sound,
I can pull things off the ground.

With all my might,
I will give you a fright.

I can be scary and strong,
You will always get me wrong.

For I am a . . .

Ben Harrison (11)
All Saints CE Primary School

DEATH

Death is red-hot,
It smells like lava,
It tastes like rotten sweets,
It sounds like rubbish crunching,
It feels like hard glass,
It lives in the middle of a cave.

Samantha Over (10)
All Saints CE Primary School

Chameleon

The chameleon sits grumpily on his branch,
Bright green, bobbly skin camouflages him in the jungle.

Its back, beady eyes jerk back and forth independently,
His long, sticky tongue waiting to pounce,
Its three long horns are like a triceratops.

Prey!

With one of his beady eyes he spots a hovering insect,
In a split second his tongue pounces on it, like a cheetah,
His chainsaw teeth bite through it.

Its swirly lollipop tail curls and uncurls as he crawls back miserably,
Like a grumpy, old granny.

'Boring insect!' he grumbles, 'nothing is exciting in my life!
Everything's boring! Grump!'

Michael Powell (11)
All Saints CE Primary School

A Storm

A sky lighter,
A people frighter,
A rumble of thunder,
A people plunder,
A housewrecker,
A puller of a double-decker.

A catalogue to make me
The storm!

Daniel Turner (10)
All Saints CE Primary School

Porcupine

I can fight like a knight,
I can dig like a mole,
I can rattle my tail
And I live in a hole.

I can bite like a mite,
I can scratch like a cat,
I can prickle my enemy
And I'm as swift as a bat.

I can fight like a porcupine,
I can dig like a porcupine,
I can rattle my tail,
For I am a porcupine.

Oliver Perratt (11)
All Saints CE Primary School

Walrus

Big, fat, wrinkled body,
Like a curled up sack,
Sitting there, waiting.
Big, flat nose,
Smelling the fish,
The long, sharp tusks hanging
From his drooping down, dumb mouth.
Like a puppet,
Like a melting ice cream,
The walrus would groan
'My food is here.'

Todd Larcombe (12)
All Saints CE Primary School

A Cat

A mouse catcher,
A perfect pouncer,

A ball chaser,
A fast racer,

A chair climber,
A dog hater.

Charlotte Goodwin (10)
All Saints CE Primary School

Something Lurking

I woke up on a dark and gloomy morning.
The stars are still twinkling against the moonlight.
I can hear my mum and dad still snoring, so loudly.
Suddenly the post comes through our cold, damp door.
It startles me, so I get out of my warm, cuddly and squidgy bed.
I open the very creaky door.
I walk slowly down the old broken stairs. I stop.
Listen I can hear something.
I can hear something moaning.
I stop. I bend over. I turn around.
It's there, standing there growling, I can't bear it.
It is green and slimy with snot hanging from its nose.
It's left a trail of slime behind it.
I grab the post, turn and run.
I jump into my bed, pull the duvet over my head.
Morning dawns and Mum is picking up the post,
I go downstairs, there is no slime on the carpet . . .

Katie Lenton (10)
Awliscombe CE Primary School

FRIENDS

I used to wish I had a friend
A friend to help me by,
Someone whom I could depend on
Someone who would not lie.

I used to wish I had a friend
A friend whom I could love
Someone who I could talk to
Someone who would not talk about me.

I feel lonely and grey
This is a horrid day
I think I have found one friend
His name is Jess.

Jess is a cat
I think he feels friendless,
I whisper in his ear
'Will you be my friend?'

He miaows a quiet miaow,
I think this means yes,
I give Jess a cuddle
Thinking he's the best.

Now I have found my friend
We will never part
You're my best friend ever Jess
Even though you have paws!

Sian Hawkins (9)
Awliscombe CE Primary School

THE BIG BLUE OCEAN

The big blue ocean,
As silent as a summer's day
As rough as a tornado
Running wild
Where a giant's hand rushes across the land.

Full of life
Full of care
So gentle
So dangerous everywhere.

There are all sorts of creatures,
In that big blue world.
Big fish, small fish, everywhere.

Not just fish,
But crabs, jellyfish and octopus,
All sorts of animals.
Some are gentle,
Some bite!
But that is what makes
The ocean what it is.

Ceri Ashford (10)
Awliscombe CE Primary School

MY TEACHERS

My teachers are funny,
They tell good jokes,
And they cheer us up
When days are grey.

My teachers have money,
They buy new books,
Water colours and crayons,
Even sweets at the end of term.

My teachers are people too,
They are very honest
And help us with our tables,
They're just like my friends.

My teachers are like weather,
Sometimes they're stormy,
Sometimes they're calm,
Sometimes they bring the sunshine.

Hannah Smith (10)
Awliscombe CE Primary School

GRANDAD'S DEAD

I hear my mum,
Yes, she's back,
Is it good news?
I really hope it is!
I run to hear,
Oh no,
Bad news,
She's crying.
Nanny turns the tap on,
I look at the rushing, spitting water,
I feel like my life is the water,
Running down the drain.
Grandad's dead,
I can't believe it,
I feel like
My life has been torn in two halves.
Why?
Why, I ask is it me?
Is there a curse on my family?
I will never know.

Tanya Summers (10)
Awliscombe CE Primary School

THE BOY

The sad, neglected boy drops his skull in affliction
His mother screams 'Get out of this house you revolting worm'
The boy's heart crumbles into infinitesimal pieces
As his father rears his fist to his mother's face
The boy wishes that the world would dissolve
And he would decrease into a compact puddle.

There was an earthquake,
The earthquake cleared the boy's house in half.
His mother and father have to hold hands
To pull each other over the other side.
The father pulls the mother closer and closer
Until love and devotion spreads.

Matthew Marks (9)
Awliscombe CE Primary School

MY BUNNY

My bunny was pure,
black fur was silky soft.
I loved to touch her fur, day after day,
just to feel in Heaven.
She loved to prance around and play
and sometimes felt I was smiling.
She was as big as a baby rhino
and I found it funny
when people teased me about it.
My dog liked to watch her as well,
but now she's gone.
Escaped?

Alice Quick (11)
Awliscombe CE Primary School

My Teacher

My teacher is fun and funny
She takes us on trips to places
Where I never thought I would go.
She makes us laugh,
She lets us listen to pop music.
Like 'Now 50' or 'Now 49'.
Sometimes she lets us
Do double art lessons.
My teacher is very kind
But sometimes she can be really strict.
I really like my teacher
She is really cool!
Her name is Mrs Allen
And she makes us giggle and laugh.
I really love my teacher
And I'll miss her when I go!

Fern Jeffrey (10)
Awliscombe CE Primary School

Hide-And-Seek

The first place I look is downstairs,
I can't find him anywhere.
Not in the loo
Not outside too.
I look behind the shelf
He is not with the cobwebs.
He is not in the dark under my bed,
I don't know where to look.
Why don't I look behind me?
He is there.

Tony Paul (10)
Awliscombe CE Primary School

The Sea

The wind is swaying through my hair,
I'm standing on the beach.
The shells are cracking under my feet,
I'm running along the beach.

The waves are tingling up my legs,
I'm swimming in the sea.
The salty water's knotting my hair,
I'm diving into the sea.

The fish are swimming all around,
I'm fishing from the pier.
The crabs and lobsters dig deep in the sand,
I'm dozing on the pier.

The people are claiming all the beach,
I'm weeping in the sand.
The children spread out their towels,
I'm upset, the beach is mine.

Tilley Vanstone (10)
Awliscombe CE Primary School

The Sea

From the calmest bays
To the wrath of the open ocean
The sea is always changing.
From the freezing and dark seas from the north
To the warm and light seas of the Equator
The sea is always changing.

From the murky and bottomless oceans
To the transparent and shallow Mediterranean
The sea is always changing.
From the angelfish of the deep
To the mullet in Devon's marinas
The sea is always changing.

Ross Boulton (11)
Awliscombe CE Primary School

PONIES

My wish is to have a pony,
My pony would be chestnut and called Jonie.
I dream 'bout cantering in a field,
The sun setting, the wind.

My wish is to have a pony,
My pony would be grey and smoky,
I would jump the jumps
And run the fields.

It would be my best friend,
I would take care of it all day
If you let me save up?
I'll help you with your chores,
It would be my love and joy,
So how about it?
Just for meeeeee!

Katy Braddick (10)
Awliscombe CE Primary School

My First Day Of School

It was my first day of school
I was in the car looking out of the scary window.
I had a really funny feeling inside
Like a *monster* was getting me.
When I looked at the school
It was like a massive giant was getting me.
Then I looked down at the kids playing,
They were like the small people
Running away from the *evil giant*.
It was time to go to class
I looked at the class . . . *scary.*
When it was time to go home
I got quite excited.

Sophie Boland (10)
Awliscombe CE Primary School

My Teddy

I have a teddy who's nine years old
I sleep with him when I'm very cold.
When I get a bad dream at night,
When I'm sad I cuddle him tight.
When somebody's died I cuddle him to the break of day,
Because I will never see that person again.
I love my teddy, I take him everywhere.

My teddy looks very cute
In his mini sparkly suit,
From the playing, the stitching loops
And so his own arm droops.

Natasha Boland (9)
Awliscombe CE Primary School

Twisters

Twister
An angry monster,
Appears in the sky,
Tears apart a house,
Racing towards me,
'Ah, Dad help!'

Tornado
A mad monster,
Appears in the sky,
It picks up a house,
Juggles with it,
Then throws it away like an old toy.

Hurricane
A furious monster,
Appears in the sky,
Swallows up a house,
It plays with a car like it's a toy,
'Please help me!'

Thomas King (11)
Awliscombe CE Primary School

Spring

The sun is up in the sky,
The birds are on the wing.
Winter is gone, spring is here
And the birds start to sing.
The flowers are in bloom,
The trees are in blossom,
The wind blows through my hair.

David Atkins (10)
Awliscombe CE Primary School

A Summer's Day

On one beautiful summer's day
When the sun was blazing
Blazing on the blue ocean
The ocean was sparkling.

On the beach
Sand looked gold.

The trees were rich
Birds here and there
Bright blue sky
Shining clouds
The wind is gentle.

All the workmen having lunch
All the farmers resting quiet
What a summer's day.

Benjamin Baker (10)
Awliscombe CE Primary School

My Teacher

My teacher is nice and really kind.
She helps me with my work.
She's good, funny and kind.
I hope she never leaves.
I don't want to go in September but I do.
Why? Why? Why?
I hope I see her before we go.
I like Mrs Allen.
I will never forget her when I go away.

Ursula Clarke (11)
Awliscombe CE Primary School

Moving School

Have you ever moved school?
If you have you know how I feel.
It is the sweltering summer of 2000.
It is the summer holidays again.
They have come round so fast.
I am, or was, year three.
I am lying awake in bed.
It is 5am.
The clock is ticking my time in Winchester away.
I hear Julia turn over in her bedroom.
I creep silently over to the window.
I climb onto the window sill and look out on the street.
I see the moon reflect on our slide.
I sit there for a while.
Then I hear my alarm go off.
We have to leave so early.
I munch my toast as the car zooms along the A303.
I think about all my friends I'm leaving,
The park down the road and the school.

On my first day at my new school I'm as nervous as a lamb.
I make friends and enemies quickly.
I miss Winchester,
But I will never forget that place.

Joel Russell (9)
Awliscombe CE Primary School

My Big Dread

I trudged through the school doors
Hoping the teacher won't set a test.
My worst Monday morning moment
Was right at this second.
I walked through the door,
The others could feel my dread.
I sat and slouched in my chair,
Miserably waiting for my bore.
The teacher came bounding
Through the classroom door
And the words I sadly anticipate
Were the first to come out of her mouth.
'The test of the term'
My eyes were filling up with fury.
She lay the test in front of my eyes
With a wicked look.
My brain was teasing.
My eyes were streaming.
The clock was ticking,
My test past my brain.
The test was over,
It seemed like seconds.
I poked my nose into my book,
Waiting for my grade
For the first time I got an A+
But I still have the dread
Of history this afternoon.

Tanya Broom (10)
Awliscombe CE Primary School

RAIN, SUN AND THE WIND

Rain patters on the window,
Splish, splish, splash,
The rain is getting harder,
Always getting harder,
Splatter, splatter, splatter,
The rain is now flooding the road,
Always getting deeper,
Swish, swish, swish,
There goes a car,
The rain has stopped.

The sun is coming out,
It is getting brighter,
Always getting brighter,
Sunrays appear,
They're always getting stronger,
All the water is disappearing,
The sun is setting,
Setting in the west of the sky.

It is night now,
The wind is coming,
It will be coming soon,
Here it is, rushing past the window,
The wind is getting stronger,
Always getting stronger,
It is beating on the window,
It is dying down,
Getting weaker,
Always getting weaker.

Emma Matthews (10)
Awliscombe CE Primary School

NIGHT

The sun is falling
Night is here
The moon has come
Shining, shining
The stars are twinkling
High in the sky
Like planets
Far away
The night goes on
Never-ending darkness.

All the people are in their beds
Sleeping, sleeping
Something's moving
Down below
The badgers are out
Hunting for food
So are the foxes
Sly and slick
The owl is hooting
In the sky
He found a mouse
He's going to get it.

He dives down quick
He's got his dinner
Goes back home
For the sun is rising
Day again
Let's go to school
And play.

Emma Surridge (10)
Awliscombe CE Primary School

SEASONS

Spring
Spring is that time of year
When animals and plants are growing.
Lambs and birds start their life happily
When flowers are sprouting and summer is coming.

Summer
Summer is an exciting season
When children are out playing
Nights are getting lighter
Days are getting longer
Summer is a season which everybody likes.

Autumn
Leaves are falling
Nearing the time to winter
Gardens are full of leaves
Dark nights are drawing in
Fires are lit, nice and cosy.

Winter
Winter is a season of excitement
Christmas is on its way
Children are getting excited along the way
Christmas Eve is a night for wishes
Children are tucked up in bed,
But soon it will be spring again.

Charlotte Witt (10)
Awliscombe CE Primary School

TREASURE

Treasure . . .what does it means to me?

Rubies and diamonds
Emeralds and gold
Amethyst and silver,
Sapphire I'm told
Under the ground
Beneath a tree
Really you will soon see
Excited I am, what will it be?
When I open the chest

There's nothing for me!

Sophie Jeffries (9)
Combe Martin Primary School

HIDDEN TREASURE

Hanging from my tree,
I can see the clear blue ocean,
I dropped to the ground
And landed in a mound,
A box was uncovered,
There to my great delight
It was all sparkling bright.
Red, gold and silver
I can live forever.

Ben Lawson (9)
Combe Martin Primary School

HIDDEN TREASURE

She is my hidden treasure, the one I love,
She's always very kind to me
And never impolite.

Yes, she is my mum,
She buys me sweets
When I'm glum.

She's very sweet
And considerate of me
And other people.

So this is a poem about my mum,
To make her feel warm,
I love her, very much.

Samantha Wells (9)
Combe Martin Primary School

HIDDEN TREASURES

There's treasure under the frothy, foamy waves,
where the hermit crab comes out to sing
and the dolphin comes to dance.
The mermaid with her long red hair and angelic face,
they have a party to celebrate
finding the treasure.
There was a crown in the chest
so they dethroned the most beautiful Ariel,
the mermaid queen.

Maria Johns (10)
Combe Martin Primary School

Searching For Buried Treasure

With my metal detector I search around
To see what is buried in the ground
Gold or silver I don't care
Even jewellery for me to wear
I walk up and down on the land
I even walk on the sand
I get excited when I hear my detector sound
I start to wonder what I've found
With my trowel I dig in the soil,
But all I find is a piece of foil
One day I would love to find some buried treasure
If I did it would give me great pleasure.

Darren White (9)
Combe Martin Primary School

As I Was Walking

As I was walking
I heard someone talking
Over the top of the gulls squawking

I looked at my feet
And gave a great squeak
For there an oyster did lay

I opened it up and had a great shock
As there was a glistening pearl.

Nathaniel Carter (10)
Combe Martin Primary School

Hidden Treasures

He comes on a Monday in a very big van
Most people know him as the recycling man
I shouted to ask him, 'Do I have to pay?'
He said, 'No, I'll be happy to take your treasures away.'

We squashed bottles and cola cans
Out ready for the recycling man
We stamped and crushed and bashed and beat
We worked so hard we had sore feet.

We filled the green bag with clothes and shoes
Mummy and Daddy did not know who's
The man next door did not grin
Because we put his washing in.

Treasures come in many ways
Not always how you think these days
So remember before you trash that tin
Think of the future
The recycling bin!

Rosie Collins (8)
Combe Martin Primary School

Down In The Cellar

Somewhere down in the cellar one day
While the rest of the world were sleeping
The mice and rats came out to play, jumping around,
Because this was their day.

They jumped over boxes full of hidden treasure,
They weren't aware, they didn't care,
They just enjoyed their pleasure.

Hannah Lovering (11)
Combe Martin Primary School

Farm

It was that time again, time for an adventure!
Stomp, stomp, squelched our boots
As we walked through the fresh cowpat.
When we saw a bottle short and fat.
We opened the bottle to find a map,
Which had on it how to find a treasure cap!
We looked at the map for a while,
Then our faces filled with a smile!
We found where the treasure was hidden
Deep in the ground
We dug and dug and dug some more
We found the cap and ran back home
Chased by an angry looking gnome!

Daniel Bowden (9)
Combe Martin Primary School

Hidden Treasures

Treasures are gold,
They can be sold
They sometimes look old

Treasures can be found on beaches
Hidden in the sand or on watery land

Hidden treasures are made of metal
Just like a kettle

Hidden treasures can be found
In a chest towards the west

Pirates find hidden treasure about
And take them to their hideout.

Melissa Spencer (10)
Combe Martin Primary School

TREASURE

Hidden treasure on the beach,
Stacks of gold coins and rubies,
Pirates fighting for the treasure,
Cannons, pistols, bang! Bang!
Look at that treasure map,
Captain says, 'Find that treasure,'
Over the seas and bounding waves,
No sight of treasure yet,
Yes on land again, that's better,
Search every nook and cranny,
Not yet Captain.
Found it!

Sam Hughes (8)
Combe Martin Primary School

HIDDEN TREASURES

The sea is a cave of moulded blue,
Stood up by a crossbones flag,
The sea monster stands upon his deck,
Dreaming of his wildest desire, treasure.
He leaves footsteps on the golden sand,
Digging for his dream, diamonds and gold,
He sails across the moulded sea,
To share his wounded find.

Michelle Townson (9)
Combe Martin Primary School

Untitled

As I walked past their table,
I catch bits of their conversation,
She,
Her,
Can't,
Won't,
I try to fix them together,
But I can't,
I don't want to,
At play time wanting to join in their games,
To wear their clothes,
Looking,
Staring,
They're looking at me,
I think . . .
They're coming towards me,
I know!
But all they do is push past me with a sly look.
It looks like I'm still on the outside, trying to get in.

Sylvie Pinder-White (10)
Drake's School

Riddle

It comes out in the morning,
As it comes out
The colour is like a warm fire
It disappears
Leaving a dark hole
What am I?

The sun.

India Loy (9)
Drake's School

CAN I GET IN SOME WAY?

I can't be a snake because . . .
I can't slither along on the ground,
I can't spit poison at eyes.

I can't be a lizard because . . .
I can't climb high in the trees,
And I can't make my skin scaly.

I can't be a chameleon because . . .
I can't put out my tongue to catch a fly.

I can't be starling because . . .
I can't sing beautiful harmonies
And I can't flutter in the air.

I can't do anything!
But I try so hard!
I try to go up to animals and stroke them,
But no, they just run away or fly.

I try so hard,
Can I get in some way?
But no . . . I'm still an outsider in their world.

Daniel Carpenter (10)
Drake's School

THE DEEP BLUE SEA

The deep blue sea, still
then rocking, people swimming,
boats cutting through the water,
high waves, growing
knocking people off their surfboards,
people drowning.

Amy Urry (10)
Drake's School

Untitled

I am white and furry
I live in the high, cold, snowy mountains,
If I saw a human I would probably eat them
And leave the bones . . .
I hate seeing light,
And I have no friends,
I cry when I am alone,
I want friends.

But I get so hungry
I eat my visitors
Some people try to catch me with a bear trap.
Nobody has seen me
And I go down the mountain again
I normally see wolves at night
Howling at the moon
But when I'm sleeping
I eat them and then
Nobody disturbs me . . .

Who am I you ask?
I am . . . *the yeti.*

Joshua Edwards (9)
Drake's School

Dolphins

They like to play a lot with others
They are my favourite type of creature
They live deep down in the blue sea
They lighten up the day for me.
They love people.

Louise Richards (10)
Drake's School

A Great, Big Puddle Of Water

A great, big puddle of water
sitting there, by itself
doing nothing, nothing at all.
Wait a minute, there are more
drops of rain falling
from the sky, splish, splash!
As they fall from the sky
suddenly the rain has stopped!
The sun has just come out
then dries up all of the puddles
from the wet ground.
Now they are all gone!

Zara Urry (10)
Drake's School

Shape Poem

I shine like a diamond in the sky.
In the dark space
I'm full of gas
I'm a sizzling ball of fire
I brighten up the sky
No one can feel me
I'm blazing hot.

Callum Gamble (10)
Drake's School

A Sight For Sore Eyes

One frosty winter morning
Just as the day was dawning

I jumped out of bed
And bumped my head

The stars in my eyes went round and round
Then it was time to walk my hound

We walked along the icy street
There upon we chanced to meet

There before my very eyes
Why! It was a *yeti* eating fries

My dog took flight at such a sight
And disappeared until the night.

Hayley Alford (9)
Feniton CE Primary School

Vampires

Vampires like to suck blood!
Vampires like to have a bath of mud!
Vampires eat eyeballs and meat,
that you have stepped on with your feet!
Vampires love witches who live in ditches!
Vampires eat berries that have been squashed by cherries.
Vampires sleep beneath the moon.
Vampires eat golden blood with a spoon.
Vampires dance at the ball!
Vampires like to play at nightfall!

Olivia Kennaway (8)
Feniton CE Primary School

ANIMALS

The cat
was walking along the mat
wearing a hat.

The dog
was walking through the fog
watching a frog.

The mouse
was creeping
through the house.

The pig
was dancing in a jig
picking up a twig.

The bird
was seen,
but not heard.

The cow
did a lovely little bow
after a little girl showed her how.

The sheep
was asleep
while the pig had a quick peep.

Isabel Stribling (8)
Feniton CE Primary School

Pygmies, Palms And Pirates

Of pygmies, palms and pirates,
Of islands and lagoons,
Of blood-bespotted frigates,
Of crags and octoroons,
Of whales and sunken ships,
Of quicksands, cold like coal,
My mother's broken lips,
Are just like a halved soul.
Of barley, corn and furrows,
Of farms and turf that heaves,
Of rabbits, ghostly burrows,
When lights on summer eve,
They burn so shiny green and red,
So all the pirates stay in bed,
So please look out for ghosts and pirates,
Or else they'll come and get you.

Zhyna Charmayne Christopher (9)
Feniton CE Primary School

Me And My Sister

Me and my sister shout at each other.

Me and my sister whine.

Me and my sister say, 'Oh bother!'
When I have six sweets and my sister has nine.

Me and my sister start to sigh.

Me and my sister tell my mother of each other
and then she says, 'Why, oh why?'

By the way, I am the angel.

Sarah Doyle (10)
Fremington Community Primary School

The Forgotten Garden

The Andrews' used to live there,
They lived their life without a care.
But until they moved away
I haven't seen them from that day.
The grass has grown waist-high
Roses climbing to the sky.
Rusty, old swing covered in ivy,
Nothing in this garden is ever tidy.
Benches rotting with the rain,
Most people think it is a shame.
Alpines spreading all over the place,
But to them it's a spreading race!
Trees growing so tall,
Listening to the wind's call.
Old, grey brick-stone wall
Looking as if it's going to fall.
All behind a wooden door
Their secrets would stay there forever more.
Now it's got someone to love and care
And you'll see her secrets there.

Jemma Collins (10)
Fremington Community Primary School

Dolphins

Down in the deep, deep sea
On top of the rocks dolphins want to be
Little lions swimming in the sea
People say she's the one that I want to be
Her fins are wavy like me
Never going away for her tea.

Lisa Beer (9)
Fremington Community Primary School

THE CAT, DOG AND RAT

Once there was a cat,
Who lived under the mat.
The cat drank water from the tap,
Then sat on his owner's lap.
Once there was a dog,
Who sat outside on a log.
The dog thought the log was awake,
But it was really floating in a lake! Aaagh!
Once there was a rat,
Who lived under the mat with the cat.
They all took buns out
Into the sun and had fun.
They jumped onto the log
And there they still are in the lake!

Matthew Huxtable (8)
Fremington Community Primary School

ALL ABOUT ME

I live in a house
By the sea
I hate you
And I don't hate me!

I live by my friend
Opposite the park
My friend's got a brother
And he's called Mark.

I live near my enemy
She's so yucky
She eats beans
And she's so mucky.

Catherine Sankey (9)
Fremington Community Primary School

Slithering Snake

Swiftly slithering,
sliding like no small, slippery snake
has ever gone before.
Through the rocky canyon, out the rocky cave
through the boiling desert sand
drinking from the oasis.

As he slithers along
hunting for his prey
he nabs them
he jabs them and slaughters them
sheds his skin while slithering.

Joshua Cornewall-Walker (10)
Lady Seaward's CE Primary School

Strawberries

Juicy, fresh, sweet, ripe, red strawberries
Sweet, ripe, red, juicy, fresh strawberries
Fresh, juicy, ripe, sweet, red strawberries
Red, ripe, sweet, fresh, juicy strawberries
Ripe, red, juicy, fresh, sweet strawberries
With sugar is how we like them most!

Zoe Moss & Charlotte Bird (9)
Lady Seaward's CE Primary School

Man-Eating Crocodile

Flicking legs swimming
Big jaws killing

Fat body slamming
Powerful eyes scanning

Small feet paddling
Scaly skin slithering

Huge belly panting
Man-eating crocodile hunting.

James Gold-Lewis (9)
Lady Seaward's CE Primary School

Kelly Kangaroo

The biggest ever woolly pouch
Was worn by Kelly Kangaroo.
She bounced around the dusty plain
Until her home became a zoo.
Then one day a Joey came
A bouncy footed friend
He lived a happy, grateful life
And drove us round the bend!

Sophie White (10)
Lady Seaward's CE Primary School

The Search For Water

Lost in the desert,
On camel back,
Rides a thin man
The search for water.

Golden sand lies everywhere,
Like a sleeping cat,
The sun is burning,
The search for water.

Lizard lies on the rock,
Runs at the sound,
It's only camel snorting,
The search for water.

Man jumps off,
Shouts in the air,
'I've found it!'
He's found the water!

Josie Rylands (8)
Lydford CP School

Autumn

It's autumn time again,
Down comes the rain.
Days are getting shorter
Because year's in the last quarter.
The weather is getting colder,
Especially if you're older.

Kerry Crocker (9)
Lydford CP School

Save The Children

When you see all the hungry children,
You want to help in every possible way.
But then you want to scream and shout at the cruelty,
But you just have to say.

Help the hungry children
In all the poor places
Don't just look at the little, starving faces.
We're gonna work together,
To help them, all of the children
We're gonna work together.
To set them free
We're gonna work together.

We're lucky to have
All the things that we own,
But they are so unfortunate, all alone,
But when we rise,
We'll give them all they've wanted
Yeah.

Help the hungry children
In all the poor places
Don't just look at the little, starving faces.
We're gonna work together,
To help them, all of the children
We're gonna work together.
To set them free
We're gonna work together.

Take food
Praise the children
Be good
Help the children
We're all gonna *save the children!*

Help the hungry children
In all the poor places
Don't just look at the little, starving faces.
We're gonna work together,
To help them, all of the children
We're gonna work together.
To set them free
We're gonna work together.

Help the hungry children
In all the poor places
Don't just look at the little, starving faces.
We're gonna work together,
To help them, all of the children
We're gonna work together.
To set them free
We're gonna work together.

Margot Douglas (11)
Lydford CP School

TRAVEL

Fly to Spain,
I can't wait.
There's my shoes
With my case
Here's my dad
Start the car.
There comes Mum
Let's go far.

Luke Crocker (10)
Lydford CP School

Seasonal Haiku

Spring
Spring is here again.
Crocuses smelling sweetly.
Birds sing daintily.

Summer
Summer is with us.
Beaches all packed with people.
Wonderful sunshine.

Autumn
Autumn leaves fall down.
Leaves go crunch under my feet.
Blackberries are ripe.

Winter
Winter snow drifts down.
Snowdrops in the garden bloom.
Frost is all around.

Olivia Duff (10)
Lydford CP School

Place To Place

Place to place
Place to place
How do I get there?
A running race.

Bus to train,
Train to plane
How do I get there?
It's a pain.

Scooter to bike
Bike to car
How do I get there?
I'm going to Par.

Robert McClelland (9)
Lydford CP School

AUTUMN DAYS

Autumn days when raspberries grow bright and slow,
Through the air and the breeze is the chill of a lifetime.

The soft, smooth silk laid quietly inside the chestnut,
The golden corn is waving in the field, ready to cut.

The frill inside the spider's web with sparkles waiting ahead,
The vegetables laid out on tables soon will be given to the stables.

The clock is falling backwards because winter is now near.
The trees start to rumble as tractors come closer and closer.

The flowers are starting to get ready for their long sleep
They are going to grow as deep as they can go.

Weather goes and everyday may be older and windier
When rain comes it makes fields muddy.

Thank the sun and thank the rain for the good they bring
The rain was good for the drink it gave people and animals.

Thank you sun for the warmth it gives us
And the lightness it lets us have.

Some animals change the colour of their skin to white
Give good life to all creatures alive at autumn time.

Kym Peacock
Lydford CP School

If You Ever See A Goblin

If you ever see a goblin, this is what to do,
Shout and scream because I haven't got a clue.

But I know some things about goblins that might come in handy,
I'll start with things they hate, it's things that are wet or sandy.

It is rather simple, everyone knows,
That they have twelve fat fingers, twelve fat toes, two tiny eyes
and one very long nose.

But if you ever see a goblin this is what to do,
Shout and scream because I haven't got a clue.

It doesn't stop there, I have some other things as well,
Like they don't have normal heads, they're shaped like a bell.

If you want to know something about their belly,
I will tell you this, but only once, it's like a big, wobbly jelly.

If you ever see a goblin this is what to do,
Shout and scream because I haven't got a clue.

But if you ever see a goblin and he asks you to play,
Take my advice, run right away.

Chloe Richards (9)
Montgomery Combined School

The Owl

Sitting listening, nothing's there
Sound can be heard from afar
Though nothing seems to be around
Waiting for the slightest sound,
But soon it can be found.

Ian Hutchinson (11)
Montgomery Combined School

Fearsome Forest

Foxes howling, growling,
Owls hooting
Heart thumping
Leaves rustling,
I'm scared stiff.
Nowhere to run
Nowhere to hide
Wind blowing,
I've got chills down my spine,
My mind's racing
I can't go back
Got to carry on
Trees looming high above me
I am petrified.

Chelsea Whatling (11)
Montgomery Combined School

The Fear Of The Forest!

A dark, shimmering forest stands before me,
Owls hooting and tooting,
Foxes howling and growling,
Trees stare down at me,
'Is anyone there?' I ask.
Heart pounding,
Chills running down my back,
Struggling to run, I fall.
Laying there I hear whispers,
Trees, ten feet tall, growing and cowering in the wind,
I get up and find I'm lost!

Abigail Stubbs (11)
Montgomery Combined School

Silence, Sweet Silence . . .

Silence, sweet silence,
Is there such a thing?

Chairs scraping the floor,
Footsteps creeping along the corridor,
Tapping on the table.

Silence - shhh.

Birds softly singing,
Radiator strangely clicking,
Clock quickly ticking.

Silence - shhh.

Wind tingling in the air,
Classes chattering over there,
People sniffing and snuffling.

Silence - shhh.

Silence, sweet silence,
Is there such a thing?

Parisa Pourhabib (11)
Montgomery Combined School

Hockey

H itting the ball really fast
O pening the chances to score
C ontrolling the ball well
K icking the ball out of the goal by a goalkeeper
E njoying the game as much as possible
Y our skills helping the other score.

Joe Hitchcock (10)
Montgomery Combined School

Leopard

The leopard stands still waiting, waiting
so still, so sleek.

There's a rustle in the bush, an antelope puts its head around the corner
and starts to run, run, run.
The leopard still waiting, waiting
so still, so sleek.

The leopard pulls the antelope to its bloody death
it's blood dripping, dripping, dripping.

The leopard stands still, waiting, waiting
so still, so sleek.

It finishes its meal for the day,
but its spotted robe is mangled in blood,
the blood of the antelope.

The leopard stands still, waiting, waiting
so still, so sleek.

Laura Lambert (12)
Montgomery Combined School

Fire

Fire burns through the barn
Fire crackles far and near,
The fire's near, horses fear
Fires burning beside you.

Jade Young (9)
Montgomery Combined School

The Twelve Months In A Year

January brings a glow to your cheeks.
February brings a chill to your toes.
March brings a cleaning frenzy.
April brings more than a shower.
May brings out the buds of spring.
June brings the sun upon us.
July brings the summer all together.
August brings the barbecue burning.
September brings children a new turning.
October brings sweets and treats.
November brings Guy Fawkes and fireworks.
December brings a cheer to our hearts.

Ayisha Govindasamy (9)
Montgomery Combined School

City Music

Snap your fingers,
Tap your feet
Step out a rhythm
Down the street.

Rap on a litter bin,
Stamp on the ground
City music is all around.

Beep says motor car,
Ding says bike
City music is what me like!

Fern Brealy (11)
Montgomery Combined School

Hidden Treasure

There's some hidden treasure at the bottom of the sea,
but let's keep it between you and me.
The waves are really soft and the seaweed is green,
but the hidden treasure is not to be seen.
Here comes the boat sailing by
run me over, say goodbye.
There's some hidden treasure at the bottom of the sea,
someone else will find it, but it won't be me.
There's some hidden treasure at the bottom of the sea,
I'm the second person to see what I can see.
Along comes a shark, I'd better fly
cause the shark's going to eat me, say goodbye.
There's some hidden treasure at the bottom of the sea,
I'm the third person to see what I can see.
Look over there is it really, could it be?
It's the hidden treasure and it's all for me!

Katie Leat (9)
Morchard Bishop CE VA Primary School

Hidden Treasure

There's some treasure in the sea,
But have we got the magic key?
Down we go deeper, deeper,
We go past the lighthouse keeper,
There goes by a jellyfish
Some people say grants a wish.
There goes a submarine
The people on it look very keen
Here comes a shark
Wave goodbye
In three seconds I'm gonna die!

Becky Collins (11)
Morchard Bishop CE VA Primary School

TREASURE

Treasure, treasure,
Beautiful treasure,
Searching for it,
Day in, day out.
Down in the mines I search,
Bashing the icy walls,
With my hammer as my axe,
My helmet on, the light shines,
In the dark, damp tunnel,
My feet are freezing with the cold and wet
My legs shake with excitement,
At last, perhaps I've found it,
A piece of shimmering, silvery gold, magnificent
Is it really treasure
Or just a sparkling stone?

Daisy Cornwall (9)
Morchard Bishop CE VA Primary School

DOOMSPELL

The Doomspell is coming in the night
Swiftly moving, clear and bright
No light, always dark
Until it slithers in the park
There it can get the power
Until the rainfall shower.
Then it goes into town
Where hopefully it will drown
Out of sight
Clear and bright.

Rose Gaskell & Beth Phillips (8)
Morchard Bishop CE VA Primary School

SPACE

Stars twinkle
Stars bright
Stars give a little light.

Moon big
Moon bright
Moon gives lots of light.

Planets big
Planets small
Planets up there but never fall!

Rockets red
Rockets blue
Rockets huge to me and you.

Aliens green
Aliens' eyes
Pickers go for me, you're very wise.

Kate Anson (9)
Morchard Bishop CE VA Primary School

DOLPHINS

Dolphins swimming
through the water.
Listen, listen to the noise.
Does it squeak?
Or does it speak?
I think it's trying to speak.
Yes!
It is speaking,
but in a different language.

Emily Hoare (8)
Musbury CP School

Under The Ocean

Under the blue ocean in the misty sea,
There is something there.
What could it be?
It's purple and big as a cloud,
What could it be?

Maybe a spider,
Maybe it's just the sea.
Is it scary?
Is it calm?
Maybe it is
Maybe it's not.

Here is a submarine.
Maybe it's just the sea
There's the monster,
Oh no, will it eat me?

I'm not in the sea
I am in my bedroom,
How could that be?
I was in the sea.
Thank goodness it was only a dream.

Jack Stephens (11)
Musbury CP School

MY FRIEND SARAH

My friend Sarah is a beautiful, bottle-nosed dolphin.
She swims through the ocean so elegantly.
She has a friend (who is a blue whale),
Her name can't be mentioned,
Never mind that!
Once she took me to the bottom of the ocean.
I tried not to be afraid of the great shark,
But it was so dark.
Soft was the sand,
So I picked it up with my hand.
Soon I found some treasure,
What a pleasure!

Danielle Herbert (8)
Musbury CP School

DOLPHINS

Dolphins swim and twirl
Right round and swim
With her friends
And with her mum and dad
We go down to the bottom
Of the sea
And I see fish
Looking at me
So I eat them!

Natasha Kerle (8)
Musbury CP School

HIDDEN TREASURES

I swim down to the bottom of the dark, blue sea
Strange colourful fish look at me.
I try not to be scared when I see a shark,
But I hardly see them because it is dark.
The sea is really cold,
But it is really old.
I dig up the sand
With my hand
And to my surprise I find a box
As mossy as a fox.
I look inside and to my surprise
I find some spies
Eating fish.

Fay Overington (9)
Musbury CP School

THE STARS

The stars are in the sky.
They shine so bright.
They only come out at night.
They glow like sparkling snow.
I'd like to fly up very high
To see the stars so very much
And I wish I could touch
Them into my hand
As they twinkle over the land.

Emily Hanley (11)
Musbury CP School

DIVING!

When I dive
I go up and down
Whee
whee
whee.
I do not drown
I spot a fish
orange and bright
it kills the light
and never says
Goodnight!

Robert Grimshaw (9)
Musbury CP School

FERRY

I love the feel of feet walking on my decks.
I shiver at the feel of water on my bow.
It's exciting to see other ships pass by.
My engine thuds steadily, bubbling under the sea.
I like fishermen waving at my excited passengers.
My name is the SeaCat.
I glide across the water prowl at night.
My sailor chains me up at night

Jonathan Ellis-Atherton (10)
Musbury CP School

FISHES

There are fish in the sea
and they are tickling me.
It's making my legs smooth,
because they were all rough before.
They like it in this sea,
because it's got a quiet shore.

Justin Holt (10)
Musbury CP School

FOOTBALL

Killing kick-off, starting the game,
Technical tackle, it hurts, what a shame.
Good goal, in the back of the net,
Yelling yellow card, one more yet,
Pinging penalty, hit the post,
Magnificent Man U, scored the most.

Leo Hinds (10)
Musbury CP School

COLOURS

Blue is the colour of the bright, blue sky.
Black is the colour of the crows, up high.
White is the colour of a huge, loud plane.
Grey is the colour of a great hurricane.
Yellow is the colour of the shiny, bright sun.
Dark blue is the colour when the day is all done.

Katie Duncombe (10)
Newport Community Primary School

My Sister

My sister is a phone freak,
She looks at it all day,
She likes to text her friends
And see what they have to say.

My sister has a CD player,
She listens to it in her room,
She sometimes turns it up so loud,
That all you can hear is boom, boom, boom.

My sister likes to go to town,
She likes to go with friends,
She comes back loaded with bags,
We're never sure how much she spends.

My sister likes to stay up late,
She never wants to go to bed,
She's always lively late at night,
But in the morning she looks half-dead.

James Bowman (11)
Newport Community Primary School

Jelly

I like jelly it wobbles in my tum
I like it more than chocolate or a burger in a bun
It is very gooey and gets stuck around my mouth
You can eat it with your finger, you can eat it with a spoon
It may have strange effects if you eat it on full moon
I threw it at the wall and all it did was fall
It comes in lots of flavours, sugar or not
I don't know how to make it so I buy it from the shop.

Simon Poile (11)
Newport Community Primary School

My Cat

Apart from a smudge of white,
She was almost all black,
We found her tied up,
In an old, brown sack.

She was hungry and skinny,
Not fat, but very thin,
And short, squeaky miaows,
Came from within.

We took her home,
And dried her fur,
And after a saucer of milk,
She began to purr.

We had to decide on a name,
Which was to be Lucky,
Then we found that she was a he,
And we called him Chucky.

All he needs is a cuddle,
Each and every day,
I love him dearly,
And he's definitely here to stay.

Lindsey Rigler (11)
Newport Community Primary School

My Cousins

Cousins, cousins I've got two
They cause me stress, they cause me pain
I wish I could flush them down the loo
I don't know how I stay sane.

They make my mum lose her hair
And drive her up the wall
Their good behaviour is very rare
I bet you don't want a cousin now at all.

Katie Rich (11)
Newport Community Primary School

MY FAMILY

My dad works in an office
Selling medicine and pills
He's always got lots of money
Until he's paid the bills.

My mum is very neat
Her handwriting's all curled
She's an amazing chef
The best one in the world.

My brother is very boring
He's on the computer all day,
But he's very good at cricket;
Especially when the ball's coming his way.

My other brother is football crazy
I'm telling you he's football mad
Sometimes he's really good
Sometimes he's really bad.

That's my family
Most of them are mad
If I didn't know them
I would be really sad.

Catherine Collier (11)
Newport Community Primary School

The Flaming Phoenix

The fire crackled softly, burning bright blue,
but then a big bang came from the flaming fireplace.
The fire raged high, huge and terrifying,
flaming, burning, raging.
As though the fire became a twisting, twirling tornado.
Then it died down revealing what it had born -
a golden, feathery mass perched upon the flames.
I gasped, 'A Phoenix!'
And with that the small, baby Phoenix took flight,
smiled and flew off at speed of light,
glimmering and glittering.
Dripping in golden flames.

Christopher Acott (10)
Newport Community Primary School

Treasure

Digging, digging all day long
Whistling to my favourite song.

Hoping I would find some gold
In the place I was told.

The chest was buried in the sand
The spade I used, hurt my hand.

I heard a voice calling me
It was Mum, 'Time for tea.'

It had all been a dream
I must have dozed off in the sun by the stream.

Jordan Bailey (10)
Newport Community Primary School

The Rock Pool

In my pool I can see another world.
Through the glass clear water under pebbles,
below me shrimps and fish are hiding from my shadow,
darting behind the shells and anemone.
We run over the rocks and down to the shore,
the surf splashing us,
the white horses spray blinding us,
our tongues tasting the salty air.
Running up the beach to the sand dunes
my hair flying in my face.
Hiding in the grass, dodging Mother,
then rolling down, down, down,
splashing back to my pool and seeing
my wild world.

Jenny Kent (11)
Newport Community Primary School

Black Bear

Black bear, black bear
stomping down the dark, dark woods
with sharp claws and a large muzzle.
We are all scared!

We're scared, we're shy,
we're tingling inside with fear.
Aaaagggh!

Dark eyes, dark nose,
sensitive ears, a sensitive nose.
Long, bulky body which can
stretch tall, relax small . . .
I am shy!

Phoebe Kent (8)
Newport Community Primary School

REFEREE!

I think that referees hate footballers
Yesterday one of my colleagues was sent off
It wasn't his fault - he was badly tackled,
But I hate referees.

I've been shown a yellow card before,
But never had a red one
The team were actually awarded a penalty,
But I still hate referees.

The ref's just blown his whistle. It's all over
3-2 was the final score
Swapping shirts with the losing team,
But I *still* hate referees.

Matthew Pincombe (9)
Newport Community Primary School

FOOTBALL

Football gives you the greatest feeling
When you can hear the crowd all cheering
Out on the pitch things are looking good
Our first goal was scored by my mate Michael Wood.
The whistle went, the ref shouted, 'Half-time.'
We were winning 12 goals to 9
The red arms raised and they all started clapping
The blues booed and hissed and then started flapping
Two minutes left
Are we going to win?
I don't believe it, our goal was in!

Stephen Ayre (9)
Newport Community Primary School

Sparkling Treasure

Treasure hidden in the earth,
Sparkling, shining, silver and gold.
Makes me richer than any king,
If I could only find it.

Treasure box, brown and dusty,
But it contains my deepest wish,
Sparkling, shining, silver and gold
If I could only find it.

Treasure shining in the sun,
Still sparkling as the moon is up.
Makes me richer than any king,
If I could only find it.

Eleanor Chamings (9)
Newport Community Primary School

Fruit

I like apples
I like grapes
I like orange cheesecake.

I like bananas
Tummy rumble
I like rhubarb in a crumble.

I like pineapple
Home I fly
I like blackberry and apple pie
Yum! Yum!

Jamie Hunt (10)
Newport Community Primary School

Polar Bear

Its eyelids are starting to now droop down,
She is trying to stay awake,
For watching all her precious cubs,
Her claw is like a rake.

It's a ferocious beast that rules the land,
Suddenly you hear a pound,
The ice has cracked into shreds,
No whisper, no roar, but a sound.

She gazes out and sees the sea,
A seal has swum right in,
A silent grab, the seal is dead,
Blood flickers on her chin.

Liam Budd (9)
Newport Community Primary School

My Cat

Daytime sleeper
Night-time creeper
Food gobbler
Hand sniffer
Tail swisher
Purr maker
Miaow giver
Tickle wanter
Space snatcher
This is my cat Tizzy.

Rebecca Southam (10)
Newport Community Primary School

My Problem

I don't know what to say,
I've been worried every day
Since my teacher said, 'At home,
I want you to write a poem.'
So I spent lots and lots of time
Trying to make words rhyme.
But I think the job is done
And it's been a lot of fun.
So, once that you have read it,
I hope that you will credit
The effort that I took,
And put this in the book!

Ellen Critchard (9)
Newport Community Primary School

Fireworks

Fireworks, fireworks in the air,
Fireworks, fireworks everywhere
Fireworks, fireworks really colourful
Fireworks, fireworks really loveable
In the air, in the night
Colourful, sparkly, nice and bright
Whizzing up at such a height
Oh what a lovely sight!

Helen Elizabeth Mackie (9)
Newport Community Primary School

Memories

I have hidden treasure inside me,
I keep them there secretly,
Everyone has treasures inside them
It doesn't have to be gold, diamonds or gems,
A memory is a great treasure to keep
Some are happy, some sad, enough to make you weep,
But whatever the memory
Good or bad, happy or sad,
They're a brilliant treasure to have,
So keep these wonderful memories,
And the wonderful treasures will keep themselves.

Emily Granger (11)
Newport Community Primary School

Hiding Places

The person who hides has a choice where to go.
They may go high, they may go low.
Would you hide on great green hilltops?
Perhaps up in old oak trees?
Tall blades of thick, lush grass
Or piles of fallen leaves?
In deep, dark forests with imaginary boars
Maybe with ponies on rocky moors?
If it's you who hides you have a choice where to go.
You might go high, you might go low.

Vicky Sallam (10)
Newport Community Primary School

Hidden Treasure

The playground is still when the children are not there,
The song of the sparrow sings,
Swings slowly swinging in the peaceful, calm wind.
Young trees sway and blossoms blooming in the lonely playground.
But, in the shade of a sweet-smelling bush
A small mouse is resting
The slowly rising sun casts its shadow across the playground
And the treasure, not broken until the children come.
As the children come to school,
The silence is broken by their laughing.
They stand still waiting for their teacher
To say they can start learning.
The bell goes and so do the children
And the treasure is there again.

Chloe Taylor (11)
Pinhoe CE Combined School

Hidden Treasure

The forest is a quiet place
In autumn it's the best
You can see the robins sleep
Whilst lying in their nest.
And in the silence of the moonlight
Dwells the spider, large and black
In the quiet of the small hours
The spider's still laid back.
And with its web winding round
The soft and mossy trees
All is calm, apart from the kind and gentle breeze.

Razna Miah (11)
Pinhoe CE Combined School

HIDDEN TREASURE

As he went towards the door
He saw what was worth living for.
He saw the world and all its beauties
The golden beauty of the sun
He saw the city edged in gold
He saw the world wake up.

As the people on the hill walked on
Before the sun was risen
He saw the sun highlight objects
Like the world had just begun
The sun was shining like a jewel
It shone like the light of the world.

Nick Shires (10)
Pinhoe CE Combined School

HIDDEN TREASURE

Deep inside the forest's core
Twisting and turning like the night before
Trickling and bubbling the stream begins.

Something lurking deep within
Diamond shapes all hopping round
Sprinkling water on the ground.

Water fairies,
Joyful with glee
Always happy as can be.

Jack Charnley (11)
Pinhoe CE Combined School

Hidden Treasure

As the house looked lone and still
Like a grandpa old and ill
The spindly branches of the tree
As still and steady as can be.
As the moon is beaming down
The tree is sparkling like a crown
As the branches of the tree
Are swaying slowly, silently.
No one knows just what you measure
When you hold the golden treasure.

As the sun slowly rises
You give away your hidden prizes
As the moon comes round once more
You are now no longer poor.

Shaun Mann (11)
Pinhoe CE Combined School

Hidden Treasure

Gentle sea breeze breathing
On the cold, wintry evening
When the blue sky was darkening
Sun was descending towards the horizon
An orange glow covered the island.
The glow sparkled on the soft sea
A wave swept onto the coral
And washed away the dirt
To reveal a shimmering block of gold.

Daniel Brown (10)
Pinhoe CE Combined School

HIDDEN TREASURE

As the traveller stepped one more
He saw behind a hidden door
Something glitter in the dark
Almost like a silver hawk.
He reached into the empty pit
And picked out something beautiful
It glistened in the gloomy dark
But then a rumbling met his ears and
Rolling boulders, spiky stones
Were bound to break his little bones.
As he drew out his mighty whip
He was sure that something he would hit,
But all he struck was the stony roof.
He ran for his life out of the cave
With a turquoise gem clenched in his fist.

Joe Skinner (10)
Pinhoe CE Combined School

HIDDEN TREASURE

Castles, forests, birds and streams,
The hidden treasures of my dreams.
I dream of a paddle boat strong and sturdy
To carry me there and back again,
Across the azure sea I glide
As dolphins twist and turn beside me,
Unknown creatures beneath the waves
Guarding treasures in hidden caves.
But all these images melt away
As the rays of sun announce the day.

Zehra Taylor (10)
Pinhoe CE Combined School

HIDDEN TREASURE

A jet-black horse rides
On this one night of the year
The moon shines like a jewel
As this black beauty is silhouetted
As it pulls and rears
With a darkened rider
His face unknown, unseen.
Ghostly hues hit worn rock and slate
The blueish blackness of the rider
Against the velvet sky.
Some say he's looking for treasure
Others say he's looking for revenge.
But no one knows - or will.

David Cranmer (11)
Pinhoe CE Combined School

HIDDEN TREASURE

The branch lay broken
As the golden, gleaming leaf
Went tumbling down . . . down,
Onto the soft and silent stream
The twig shivered
Thinking of his old friend, Leaf
Feeling that the world wasn't worth living for,
Knowing that he'd never known a friend before,
Watching his only one drift some more.

Emma Oakley (10)
Pinhoe CE Combined School

HIDDEN TREASURE

One frosty winter's day
Under the sun-caught snow
Lies a small, fluffy dormouse,
Curled up, hibernating.
He lies, woken from his dream
About golden berries
By the soft tread above him,
By the farmer ploughing his field
For the start of spring.
The mouse looks and uncurls
And digs his way out
And pulls himself up.
He looks again -
His black eyes turned to the sun.
They turn to jewels in the sun.
The deafening sound of the farmer's plough
Causes the winged birds to fly away,
Leaving the dormouse
And the farmer alone,
For another day.

Jamie Allanson (11)
Pinhoe CE Combined School

HIDDEN TREASURE

Galloping through the blazing desert
The traveller rode on his steed
He searched for golden, hidden treasure
Inside his heart was greed.

A dark, shadowy cave
Caught the lone traveller's eye
As he stamped towards the darkness
His face filled with glee.

And there the treasure was
Glistening in the shimmering moonlight
Its golden case of treasure
Sparkling in the dark gloomy cave.

Tom Scott (10)
Pinhoe CE Combined School

Hidden Treasure

The whistling wind that blew that night
Boiled up the seething sea.
My boat was thrown against the rocks
And left nearly no life in me.
I crept along the stormy shoreline
Shouting 'Is anyone there?'
But all there was, was nothingness
As far as I could stare.
I'd come to search for Golden Treasures
That no one had seen before,
But so far I'd found nothing at all
On my amazing tour.
And then I saw it sparkling there
Like a brightly-shimmering star -
Golden fruit with golden treasure
On this island afar.
The morning sun shone down from above
And filled that spot with light and love.
Beauty as well, filled that place
As the Golden Fruits had a golden taste.
These Golden Fruits had before been unknown
To the outside world,
But now a Hidden Treasure had been found -
A treasure I'd unfurled.

George Kyrke-Smith (10)
Pinhoe CE Combined School

Hidden Treasure

Deep inside, the life of a seed was stirring
As it sprouted from the ground
Its buds were starting to form.
It realised the silence of the air around
A beautiful blooming bud began to appear
And it told true beauty as summer grew near.
The fingers of the petals reached towards the sky
Hoping to hold the jewels of the sun
The life of the plant has just begun.

Sarah Dines (10)
Pinhoe CE Combined School

Splash!

My legs started to tremble,
My toes turned numb,
My arms started shaking,
'Down you go,' said Mum.

My teeth started chattering,
My eyes were popping out,
I was filled with fear,
'I'll land safely, I doubt!'

As I started zooming,
Down the huge blue slide,
I began to shout,
'Help me!' I cried.

I was going down to the bottom,
I was going to land with a crash,
I flew out of the end . . .
Splish, splosh, splash!

Megan Atkins (8)
St Andrew's Primary School, Cullompton

Swimming

I splish, splash, splosh in the swimming pool,
I dive under the deep blue shiny water,
I rise to the top, searching for air.
There are lots of noises like people
shouting, screaming and crying babies around me.
There's the fresh smell of water.
Lights that are shining green, red and yellow
like fireworks up in the sky,
make the swimming pool different colours.
People getting dizzy, people floating along
people getting wet,
people enjoying swimming.

Tessa Fenlon (7)
St Andrew's Primary School, Cullompton

The Wind

The wind rages through the trees
like dodging football players,
Chopping every last leaf on the tree
like a chainsaw, chopping the tree down.
The wind rages across the bright yellow sand.
As he washes across the sand, he reaches
up into the sky, as if he is trying to fly.
Then he zooms across the dark sea like an F1 car.
Then he rages somewhere else.

Jack Chambers (8)
St Andrew's Primary School, Cullompton

The Crystal

In some places it is crystal blue
and pricks like a pineapple.
Some bits look like the sun
and others like blueberries.
It has ten, black, tiny spots
like a Dalmatian dog.

Brendan Wood (8)
St Andrew's Primary School, Cullompton

The Obsidaw

It's smooth on one side of the rock
and cold as the rushing wind.
It's as dark as night-time and
black as coal that's in an unlit fire.

Jamie Bunden (8)
St Andrew's Primary School, Cullompton

Schorl

Hard as rock,
Black as night.
Silver like money,
Shiny and light.

Avery Fyles-Legg (7)
St Andrew's Primary School, Cullompton

Christmas Day

There are ten presents under the Christmas tree
There are nine shoved under the table
There are eight stuffed naughtily into the turkey
There are seven watching the TV cable
There are six hidden in my stocking
There are five in my bed
There are four undelivered in Santa's sack
There are three being guarded by Ted
There are two being nicked by Rudolph
The Christmas dinner's gone too
There is one angry mummy
Who is right behind me
'Oi, you!'

Jack Charles (7)
St Andrew's Primary School, Cullompton

Sapphire

White as ice,
Crystal as light
Silver and bright like a glass vase.
Shaped in a triangle
I can dream a crystal
Swimming pool filled with crystal ice
I see thought as a vase.
I can dream about this thing.

Danielle James (8)
St Andrew's Primary School, Cullompton

DUMORTIERITE

It's as tiny as a screw.
Wrinkled and jagged,
Faded and orange,
White specks and sky-blue.

It feels like dusty chalk,
With grains and marks.
It's also quite rough.
It's *Dumortierite!*

Rebecca Parker (9)
St Andrew's Primary School, Cullompton

MY DINOSAUR

My dinosaur runs like a wildcat.
He roars like the whistling wind.
He bites like a fierce lion.
He swings his tail like a strolling tiger.
His coat is as rough as my bedroom carpet.
My dinosaur's the best.

Alexander Jones (8)
St Andrew's Primary School, Cullompton

HEMATITE

Sparkly, pink,
Purple and brown.
Hard but smooth,
And glittery too.

Jessica Gatter (9)
St Andrew's Primary School, Cullompton

THE ROCK

A mud-like brown,
Green and blue on the back.
A line of silver,
Dark green on the front -
The rock.

Like a falcon's head,
With a chip on the side.
The size of a thumb,
With a dent on the top -
The rock.

Jack Southwell (8)
St Andrew's Primary School, Cullompton

THE ZOO

When I went to the zoo
The elephants stomped around and flapped their ears
The lions roared and jumped around
The rhinos charged and began to snort.

When I went to the zoo
The bats screeched and flew overhead
The flamingos danced in the shallow water
The parrots chattered to each other in loud squawks.

David Kerslake (9)
St Andrew's Primary School, Cullompton

PYROLUSITE

It's brown as a piece of
Hubba Bubba chewing gum.
It's speckled white in some places
like a falling snowflake.
It's orange at the bottom
like a fresh carrot,
and speckled black
like a dirty rubber.

Hannah Partridge (8)
St Andrew's Primary School, Cullompton

AMETHYST

It's spiky like a hedgehog,
It's as purple as a violet.
It's rough like sandpaper,
But smooth in other places.

Alexander Held (8)
St Andrew's Primary School, Cullompton

ROSE

It's a shiny and sparkly stone,
With speckles of black,
And splashes of white.
It's the colour of a pink rose.

Kirsty Herivel (8)
St Andrew's Primary School, Cullompton

The Swimming Pool

Tossing, splashing,
people diving, turning,
round and round,
children's feet mashing
in the water,
like bubbles bursting
on the ground.
Children, mums and dads
shouting like seagulls calling, crossly -
but children don't listen,
they're too busy playing.

Phoebe Meffe (8)
St Andrew's Primary School, Cullompton

Diopside

As black as coal.
As rough as a mountain.
Layers of black velvet.
A streak of lightning.

As small as an ant.
As smooth as a sword.
Stripes of a tiger.
It's a rock called . . .?

Ben Maunder (9)
St Andrew's Primary School, Cullompton

My Dog

Feed me, stroke me, cuddle me, please me,
Walk me, play with me, please don't tease me.
Take me to the field so I can run,
Take me to the baker's and buy me a bun,
Now I want to go to bed,
So I can rest my weary head,
And then I'll wake in time for tea,
And I shall need to have a wee.
After that I'd like to know
If we can have another go
I dreamt of sheep while I was asleep.
Can I now go, so I can see
If they want to play with me.
'Oh no!' it's raining, that's the end of that,
I'll have to stay here on the mat.
I know he'll take me when it stops
If he doesn't I'll start to pop!
Then Mum will say 'Oh not again
Take that dog out in the rain.'
Then I will see if she's pleased with me
When I return to mark my sheet
With my wet and dirty feet!

Joanne Gillard (7)
St Andrew's Primary School, Cullompton

Limonite

Shiny like a crystal,
Sparkly colours mixed into one.
Grey as thunder,
A speckled, wrinkly, bumpy stone.

Charlotte Smith (8)
St Andrew's Primary School, Cullompton

An Autumn Day

An autumn day is a working day,
When the farmers work and sow.
The golden leaves fall softly,
Onto the muddy ground below.

An autumn day is a windy day
When the wind blows in a gale.
The raindrops fly like a machine-gun fire,
And then comes sleet and hail.

An autumn day is a freezing day,
When frosty flowers freeze.
In houses, lights on, warm and cosy
With hot buttered bread and cheese.

Florence Browne (8)
St Andrew's Primary School, Cullompton

Sapphire

A piece of crystal,
As clear as glass.
A piece of ice,
Carved into a rectangle.

Smooth but jagged,
Grey but white.
Frozen edges
That could cut like a knife.

Amy Barney (9)
St Andrew's Primary School, Cullompton

Apalite

It's the colours of the seaside,
Sky-blue and mustard-yellow.
It's as black as coal,
And rough but smooth.
It's speckled, shiny and small.

Andrew Bird (9)
St Andrew's Primary School, Cullompton

Pyrite

It's a glamorous stone,
Glittery, silver and gold.
It's smaller than a matchbox.
Rough, bumpy and cold.

Calum Widgery (8)
St Andrew's Primary School, Cullompton

Biotite

Black as liquorice,
Sparkly as silver.
Rough but smooth,
Chipped and jagged.

Liam Webber (9)
St Andrew's Primary School, Cullompton

The Land The World Forgot

A monstrous landscape,
Storms like a whirlpool on land,
Picking up what it likes.
Penguins glide like synchronised swimmers,
Diving and rocketing on frosty shores.

Whales smash the icy waves,
Breaking blocks of ice,
Stalking microscopic krill.

Seals toboggan down the summit,
Like a skier down the slope.

Trekking down the hill,
Flying over the ice are the snow geese,
Landing in mossy grass.

Home to no one is
The land the world forgot!

James Cookson (11)
St Nicholas' RC Combined School, Exeter

Can You Survive In The Arctic?

The killing winds howling and rushing
The freezing snow brushing the people
Flicking and biting their skin
Polar bears struggling to swim in the freezing water,
The krill swimming in the deep, freezing water.
The iceberg cracks and wanders into the distance,
The cold lemmings scurrying along the soft snow,
Try and survive the long, cold winter.

Peter Stoneman (11)
St Nicholas' RC Combined School, Exeter

The Deserted Desert

Gigantic but deserted mountains of sand

Stones worn down
By the rushing wind

Gila monster staggering along with its mottled skin
Like an ancient dinosaur

The sidewinder swirling along the deserted lands
As if playing a game

Camel's humps scorched
By the sun's boiling rays

Only the Tuareg can survive
In the deserted deserts.

Emily Jones (10)
St Nicholas' RC Combined School, Exeter

The Desert

Shrubs sitting on the gritty ground,
Towering cacti with spiky thorns,
Keeping the remarkable animals out.

The sidewinder creeps away,
From the sun's ray,
And the Gila monster,
With mottled camouflaged scales.

The rushing wind deserted the desert,
And left the humid night.

Sophie Shepherd (11)
St Nicholas' RC Combined School, Exeter

In The Desert

Gigantic mountains of sand,
Shimmer in the burning sun.
Spiky armoured cacti,
Warn away food-searching animals.

Swift eagles swoop in the sky,
While lizards lumber across the crumbling rocks.

Animals hidden under the golden sand,
Armies of killer ants trooping.
The slithering scaly sidewinder,
Wriggles between the dispersing shrubs.

Scuttling scorpions searching for shelter,
Across the lonely desert.
Deserted mountains of soft sand,
Shimmer in the burning sun.

Rosalind Day (11)
St Nicholas' RC Combined School, Exeter

Winter

It is cold,
I have a shiver,
Everything's cold,
Including the river.
The coldness bites my toes,
The ice lights the moon
On a winter's night gloom.
The noise of ice on the ground
Reminds me of the cold and freezing winter.

Rebecca Curry (10)
St Nicholas' RC Combined School, Exeter

THE DESERTED DESERT

Scrubby bushes dotted down the desert,
The twisty, twirling, coiled snake,
Scuttles down the scorching sand,
Where the sun's rays shine.
Sleeping deserted place lies lonely and quiet,
Where the other animals search for their prey
The ancient Gila monster creeps silently
Down the cracked, creepy rocks.
Camels with their fattening humps
Search their way through the spiky cacti
In the boiling sand
All day long
Where will they be when the sun goes down?

Tamsin Fowles (10)
St Nicholas' RC Combined School, Exeter

THE DESERT'S SCORCHING SUN

Lizards rushing to find shelter in the sand,
Gila monsters staggering under the cacti,
Tuareg turn back on their camels,
Merciless heat!

The sand gets hotter,
Stones turn scorching,
Scorpions find shade.
Dazzling warmth!

James Lucas (10)
St Nicholas' RC Combined School, Exeter

THE BARREN DESERT

The desert dotted with scrubby bushes
No homes for miles and miles.
Tornadoes of sand twist and turn
In the blazing sunlight.

Gila monsters with mortal skin
Lumber around, under tall, proud cacti
Trying to keep out of the scorching heat.

Sidewinder rattlesnakes twist
Through the worn-down rocks
Weaving in and out of water-filled cacti.

The barren sand forming rocky towers
The hot desert winds
Bring no water to all.

Richard Wills (10)
St Nicholas' RC Combined School, Exeter

THE ARCTIC SURVIVORS

Bitter air freezes,
    Snowy blizzards have formed,
Polar bears are waiting in silence
    Huskies fight against the snowstorms,
Like the wind blowing a kite around,
    An Arctic fox creeps through the snowy morning,
Monstrous waves have frozen,
    At last the day dies down and the moon awakes!

Elizabeth Miles (11)
St Nicholas' RC Combined School, Exeter

Home To No One

Millions of scattered scrubs
Growing quietly, all alone,
Giant cacti
Protected by its thorny leaves,

The Gila monster,
Crawling and camouflaged
The sidewinder moves fast,
Sliding along.

Thousands of miles of one deserted place
Sandstorms whirling around
Blowing the blazing sand.

How can anyone survive here?

Nicholas Hoyos-Twomey (10)
St Nicholas' RC Combined School, Exeter

The Everlasting Battle

Daggers of ice stand on guard,
Winds prepare to attack,
Blizzards dart across the frost,
The vast frozen land battles,
Against a mighty force,
The death bringing coldness,
Only to be overpowered,
Once again,
Crushed by pillars of snow,
Water, just a memory,
Under the whiteness of the slippery ice,
The Arctic winds rule here!

Thomas Edwards (11)
St Nicholas' RC Combined School, Exeter

DEATH VALLEY

Everything is dry.
Nothing is wet
Scorching hot stones
On the sandy floor
Creatures everywhere
Trying to survive
When the sandstorm
Crashes in
The sidewinder
Twisting and turning
Round and round
Gila monster
With its ancient skin
Crawling to hide
In the shade
Tuareg people dodge
The sharp cacti
To find shelter
This is what the desert
Is like.

Sam Milford (10)
St Nicholas' RC Combined School, Exeter

ARCTIC SURVIVORS

The biting air freezes,
The Arctic fox dashes with the white snow
The beluga whale soars under the mystical world
The huskies are pushing against the howling blizzard
Violent icy waves camouflage the penguin's trail
The monstrous, jagged ice structures cover the land
All is silent.

Hayleigh Stedman (11)
St Nicholas' RC Combined School, Exeter

Kennings Dog

Track-sprinter
Paw-printer
Dog-napper
Log-lapper
Ball-popper
Hall-hopper
Nail-picker
Feet-licker
Cow-tripper
Couch-ripper
Tree-jumper
Night-thumper
Paddle-swimmer
Medal-winner
Man-lover
Warm-cover.

Sammy Lee (10)
St Nicholas' RC Combined School, Exeter

My Magnificent Dolphin

My dolphin is grey like the mist that hangs over the moor.
Grey like a cold winter's day.
His wail is like a horn sounding in the distance.
His fins are like knives cutting through the sea.
His tail is like a kite waving goodbye at me.
My dolphin is as active as a dog on an early morning walk.
He is like a shooting star, shining in the distance.
He resembles a ball bouncing upon the water.
I will watch over him and protect the sea in which he lives.

Naomi Hodges (9)
St Nicholas' RC Combined School, Exeter

Rainforest Rage

Leopards lie enjoying the sun's rays
As the snakes slither slyly by.
While the poison-arrow frog leaps under a tall tree for shade.
Bright coloured birds glide across the air like a rainbow.
Rainy season.

A storm erupts.
Leopards leap up the branches
Tree monkeys shelter under the roof of the forest.
Rain trickles down the lush leaves.
On every side are *giant* towering trees
And a maze of long, curling roots.
There is no life in the gigantic rainforest
Unless you know exactly where to look.

Oliver Gibbons (11)
St Nicholas' RC Combined School, Exeter

The Raging Sands

Scorching winds of sand
Shooting through the barren landscape.
The Gila monster slouching
Out from the hot cacti
Searching for something to eat.
Sidewinder snakes twisting into
The white-hot sands,
Slithering around into the forgotten desert lands
Only the Tuareg dare venture
Into the endless dangers of the desert.

Chris Mortimer (11)
St Nicholas' RC Combined School, Exeter

HOT STUFF

Scorching hot stones
Scattered around the desert.
The Tuareg people
Surviving if they can
Camels trail across
Millions of miles of boiling sand
The rattlesnake winding in
And out of the stones and scrubby bushes,
Lizards digging to find
Their shelter,
This is what the desert holds.

Jamie Brimblecombe (10)
St Nicholas' RC Combined School, Exeter

ARCTIC SURVIVORS

Northern lights shine through the morning darkness,
Howling blizzards sweep across the frozen earth,
Mighty polar bears charge through the snow,
Diving seals slide through the icy holes,
Arctic foxes scurry across the snowy ground.

Whilst we are all inside in the warm,
These amazing animals,
Are out there,
somewhere!

Jonathan Bottrell (11)
St Nicholas' RC Combined School, Exeter

THE ARCTIC SURVIVORS

Biting ice when bleak air freezes
Polar bears swim like giant dogs
Penguins cruise in the sea's bay
The Arctic fox charges through the white snow
Seals hunt in the air holes of the icy ground
Huskies pulling huge, wooden sledges up and down
the steep hills
Reindeer standing with long horns like branches
Sea is frozen like a gigantic lid
Arctic lemmings burrow into the ground
Arctic hares dig up plants
The thick, white blanket has covered up the ground
Some survive, some don't.

Becky Evans (10)
St Nicholas' RC Combined School, Exeter

ANTARCTIC SURVIVAL

Snow mountains high above the white earth
Deep ice below the bitter, frosty ground
Jagged icicles around the water's edge
Penguins waddle and dive from the icebergs

The cruel wind sweeps across the land
Blizzards are erupting
In this dismal place
How do animals survive?

Holly Keogh (10)
St Nicholas' RC Combined School, Exeter

Down In The Ocean

Down in the ocean as deep as can be,
lies a giant pirate ship,
but there's something guarding it
and it's bigger then me!

Inside the pirate ship,
a huge skeleton is there,
he wakes up with a roar,
but only when there's people near.

If you want to know
what the pirate is hiding -
then that's very clear,
a pile of treasure that he stole without fear.

Down in the ocean as deep as can be,
lies a pile of silver and gold
but there is one piece of treasure,
that is not in the pile
and do you know why?
It's because it's with me!

Jessica Gavin (9)
Sandford School

Cabbage

Cabbage is a funny veg
All crisp, round and green,
Sometimes I mistake it
For a green squashed baked bean.

Cabbage is a funny veg
All gritty, round and green,
Sometimes it speaks aloud
And floats up like a cloud.

Cabbage is a funny veg
All rough, round and bright,
Sometimes it climbs a height
And falls down very tight.

Martin Toms (8)
Sandford School

When I Grow Up

Hum, I wonder what I could be?
No, yeh! A soldier in the King's army.

I could be a doctor,
dressed in white,
to help the ill,
by day and night,
just because I'm very bright.

It will be fun to fly a plane,
and drive a very big yellow crane.

I might be a policeman very tall,
I'll be there just when you call.

I could be a funny clown,
to cheer you up when you feel down.

Now then, let me see,
most sailors I know,
go to sea,
perhaps that's what I shall be.

Now a fireman's job is a very dangerous one,
putting out fires is never fun.

There are many, many things that I could be,
I'll need a few years and then I'll see.

Davina Jewell (8)
Sandford School

Ten Little Kittens

Ten little kittens
Drinking wine
One felt sick
Then there were nine

Nine little kittens
Finding a mate
One fell in love
Then there were eight

Eight little kittens
Playing die
One went to Heaven
Then there were seven

Seven little kittens
Playing with wicks
One lit the match
Then there were six

Six little kittens
Playing with knives
One cut his paw
Then there were five

Five little kittens
Playing by the door
The door slammed closed
Then there were four

Four little kittens
Drinking tea
One burnt his tongue
Then there were three

Three little kittens
Going to the loo
One fell in
Then there were two

Two little kittens
Having fun
One tripped over
Then there was one

One little kitten
Eating a bun
He choked on a currant
Then there were none.

Joanna Crooke (9)
Sandford School

I Have A Friend

I have an imaginary friend,
His name is little Scotty,
He comes from Scotland
And he is an elf,
He is my best friend,
He goes to Scotland every month,
Sometimes he makes magic dust
And sometimes he turns me into an elf,
His friends they are wicked,
Because they are more active.

Ryan Glass (8)
Sandford School

The Emerald Of Malajorlrus

The journey begins at the two hills of Mous,
Where the heath is at its worst,
Gales blow, around the rocks.

The journey continues, past the valley of Handrus
And mountains of Hailus.
Snow storms brew, upon the caps of pure snow
And avalanches fall, to the depths of the west side.

Beyond the mountains, lies the forbidden forest where no one ventures
And the fog so thick, the trees so dead, and sharp, cut the fog.

Along the path of Jandus, you will come across the sinking marshes
And the rises of Aramel, where the myths lie.

Next, is the place of Malajorlrus, a desert land full of danger and curses.
Sitting on the top of the pyramid of the god of doom,
The emerald blazes its strong green rays
Upon the lands of Malajorlrus.

Kit Jackson (9)
Sandford School

King Of Birds

The king of birds is mighty and powerful.
He rules from a soaring sky.
He is tight-fisted and brutal to all who disobey him.
The young and old both fear him for his mighty strength.
Both humans and creatures respect the courageous eagle
Born to rule the soaring sky.

Rosie King (9)
Sandford School

My Weird Friends

Christopher Bond,
He drinks from a pond.
Edward Rice,
He's as tiny as mice.
Richard Maddock,
He bowls like Andy Caddock.
Then there's Adam Jackson,
He sings like Michael Jackson.
Simon Tietze,
Likes eating pizza.
Sam Munday,
Could be called Sam Sunday.
Matthew Bond,
He is a pond
And they are my weird friends.

Louis Kinch (9)
Sandford School

Friends

My friends are to play with,
To help me when I'm stuck.
My friends are there for me when I need them,
To talk to when I'm alone.
My friends are to have running races with,
To play games with.
My friends are to work with,
To have fun with.
My friends are to swim with,
To play sports with.

Chris Bond (10)
Sandford School

TEMPLE OF DOOM

In the temple of doom
there's lots of room
where ghosts can zoom about.

In the temple of doom
where the big, big moon
can slowly loom about.

In the temple of doom
where there's a big, big boom
exactly in the middle of noon.

So there's room, zoom
moon, loom, boom, noon
right in *the temple of doom!*

Richard Maddock (9)
Sandford School

THE FUNFAIR

The funfair is on every March and May,
when we go there, all we do is play,
we go on the roller coaster that's as tall as my house,
and it twirls round and round, like a tail of a mouse.

Then there's the roundabout and the big wheel,
the roundabout twirls round like orange peel,
the big wheel goes round with music on,
we stay there until the moon has gone.

With candyfloss all over my face,
I think I'd better leave this place,
tomorrow is another day,
when perhaps I can come back and play?

Simon Tietze (9)
Sandford School

Map

Read me, read me,
I may be old and singed, but I have a mind beyond time,
So read me and you shall see what you see.

Past the mountains, white teeth at bare cold as ice,
Keeper of the dwarves.

Past the forest, a time to tell for company is settled down,
Keeper of the elves.

Past the fiery earth of evil, a barren piece of paper full of murder
And darkness, keeper of the dark king.

Past the shire of living daylight, a shower of piety and homeliness,
Keeper of the hobbits.

There lies a hidden treasure deep in the ashen ground,
An evil belonging a ring, one ring to rule them all something
That never should be found.

Adam Jackson (9)
Sandford School

My Dog

I have a dog that never bites and chases cats.
I have a dog that loves its food and slurps its water.
I have a dog that barks at danger and is very friendly.
I have a dog that's very strong and is short and dumpy.
I have a dog that is really stubborn and is too big for its basket.
I have a dog that is too smelly and has a mind of its own.
I have a dog that is losing its sight and has a few mates.
I have a dog that is nine years old and has a golden fleece.
I have a dog that loves me.

Edward Rice (9)
Sandford School

Ashley

When Ashley is angry, she lashes out
like a demon's tail gone wild!

When Ashley is tired, she mopes about
like a bear just come out of hibernation.

When Ashley is upset, she is like
a river, just about to flood the world.

When Ashley is annoying, you want
to wrap your hands around her neck and squeeze.

When Ashley is happy, she grins like the sun
and glows cheerfully . . .

That's why I like Ashley.

Robyn Stevenson (9)
Sandford School

My Cat

My cat is a ball of fluff,
waiting to be stroked.

My cat is a dagger,
killing all the birds.

My cat is a leopard,
clawing her way up trees.

My cat is a sleeping lion,
having wonderful dreams.

That's the cat I know!

Amy Platt (9)
Sandford School

My Room

My room is red,
Like the colour of Hell.
It's the messiest in the world,
It's in the book of records you know.

My room's got a bed,
It's got a large sofa.
TV, hi-fi and a desk,
Just like Computer World.

My carpet is green,
Ceiling is white.
My light is like
A canary in flight.

My room is biggest,
Like a school playground.
Bigger than Jack's
Apart from my mum and dad's.

What's your room like?

Samuel Munday (9)
Sandford School

Lord Of The Votes

Three votes for the national SWEB energy,
Seven for the mapping in their little satellites,
Nine for the several parts of you,
One for the worst dealer of money,
One vote to have them all, one vote to end it.
One vote for Mrs Thatcher and all her stupid men.
One vote for the worst dealer of money.

Michael Snell (10)
Sandford School

Friends

My friends have curly snakes coming from their hair.
My friends have mouths the size of bats.
My friends have legs like gelatine.
My friends have ears the same as a wombat's.
My friends have noses the size of an elephant's trunk.
My friends have arms the size of a rhino.

All my friends have the same.
Snake hair,
Mouths like bats,
Legs like gelatine,
Ears like wombats,
Noses like trunks,
Arms the size of rhinos.

It doesn't matter what my friends look like,
They're all great pals anyway.

Ross Jackson (9)
Sandford School

My Dragon

My dragon is big and green,
he looks like he needs a clean,
he does smell rotten and has a big bottom
and lives in the cave of Lee.

My dragon is a sweet dragon,
even though he can be mean,
if you harm him he will burn your bum,
if you kick him he will say yum, yum, yum,
so you'd better be quick and run, run, run.

Matthew Bond (10)
Sandford School

Weather

Sun, snow, cloud, rain,
Sun, snow, cloud, rain,
Sun, snow, cloud, rain,
What will be the weather?

It might be sunny sun,
Or maybe a lot of snow.
I doubt it would be cloudy,
But imagine if it was rain!

I wonder what's the weather,
It's something I don't know,
I wish it wasn't rain,
But if it is, oh no!

We stare at the rain and eat some buns,
When we want to play in the snow,
I wish we could have some fun in the sun,
Or go out, in the clouds.

Jack Morgan (10)
Sandford School

My World

I have my special world
In the yellow end of the house.
It is extremely weird
My shop sells scrumptious things,
My play park has a swing and a scary slide.
I drive a car, a nice car, a limousine
With my beary bear
I seem to go everywhere.

Emily Lewis (9)
Sandford School

My Treasure Box

Look inside and you will find
Magic of every kind.
Wishes and whoops,
Bangs and bumps,
Of gold and purple,
Silver and blue.
Where I found it,
I do not know!
I saw it out the corner of my eye.
This box of mine is rather fine,
I could be famous one day,
And help the world . . .
All because of my box.

Lauren Boundy (8)
Sandford School

Under . . .

Under the water,
Under the sea,
Magic will happen
Around you and me.

Dolphins rise to the surface
To jump high,
Tropical fish live near the coral,
Extinct fish aren't extinct.

Under the water, under, under, under . . .
Under the sea, sea, sea, sea, sea . . .
Magic will happen
Around you and me.

Eve Daeche (9)
Sandford School

A SECRET TREASURE

A secret treasure hidden, where nobody will know,
I'm sailing on my wondrous ship rocking to and fro.
Maybe it's in the Caribbean or the coral reef,
Or perhaps in a jungle amongst those big leaves.

I want to find the treasure, I really, really do,
It's just that I've got no map, that's a problem too!
I see a weird shaped island distantly ahead,
Hooray, hooray, my luck is in, so I hugged my ted.

Looking through my telescope I shouted, 'Land ahoy!'
I rushed to the wheel and if it were a toy,
Finally my ship was there, I dropped the anchor down
I raced to the sand and found a silver crown!

I saw an 'X' and started digging, and there I saw a chest,
At last! At last! I jumped for joy, and tried to pull it open,
(tried my best)
But all I found was a photo of my family and Harry Potter books! Cool!

Vicky Munday (9)
Sandford School

HOW I FEEL

Every morning I wake up and feel tired,
Every morning when I'm at school I feel clever,
Every afternoon when I'm at home I feel like playing around,
Every evening I feel happy and cheerful,
Every evening when I'm outside I feel like swinging on my swing,
Every night when it is dark I feel scared,
Every night when I'm in bed I feel like drifting away into a dream.

Aoife Littlejohn (8)
Sandford School

My Best Friends

Vicky is a pop star,
A real singing friend.

Beth is an actress,
Her show will never end.

Helena is a model,
'You're showing off again!'

Aoife is a weatherwoman,
Forecasting the rain.

Maia is a secret agent,
A really big spy.

Molly is a parachutist,
Falling from the sky.

Jessica Symons (9)
Sandford School

Colours

Wonderful shades of blue and white,
Yellow and orange, oh so bright,
Silver colours of icy frost,
Without black and brown I am lost,
My least favourite colour is green,
Swirls of red I've never seen,
Mysterious pools of gold,
Look down as the purples unfold,
Beautiful rings of rosy pink
And many more just let me think!

Eleanor Garrett (10)
Sandford School

My Baby Sister

My baby sis is my treasure
because she's really funny.
My baby sis is my treasure
because she's dressed as a bunny.

My baby sis is my treasure
because she's really clever.
My baby sis is my treasure
because she can pull a lever.

My baby sis is my treasure
because she's really playful.
My baby sis is my treasure
because she's really joyful.

Ike Daeche (8)
Sandford School

My Parents

My parents are so good to me
You really ought to see,
They clean my room
They decorate the house.

My parents are so good to me
You really ought to see,
They feed the cats, the fish and all
They do get annoyed with me.

My parents are so good to me
You really ought to see,
They bought us a computer
They really are so kind.

Jana Webb (9)
Sandford School

Teddies

I cuddle my teddies here and there
I cuddle my teddies everywhere.

I cuddle my teddies to far places
I cuddle my teddies when I do up my laces.

I cuddle my teddies when I go on a trip
I cuddle my teddies on cars, on trains or even a ship.

I cuddle my teddies wherever I go,
I cuddle my teddies through the snow.

I cuddle my teddies when I am sad,
I cuddle my teddies when I've been bad.

I cuddle my teddies all day and all night,
I cuddle my teddies in dark or in light.

I love my teddies!

Molly Morgan (8)
Sandford School

Work

'Did you do your spellings?'
'What spellings?'

'Did you read your riddle?'
'Of course not!'

'Did you do your handwriting?'
'If you want!'

'Did you do your homework?'
'What work?'

George Lee (8)
Sandford School

Books

Books are my treasure
There are big books
Little books
L o n g books
Short books

Ha ha ho ho
Ho ho ha ha
Funny books
Ho ho ha ha
Ha ha ho ho

Weep boo hoo
Sad books

Wait a minute!
Here's a new book
It eats you!
Oh no!
Aaaaaahhhhh!

Bethany Dellamuro (8)
Sandford School

Hidden Treasure

Under the deep blue sea,
There is treasure just waiting for me,
Where the fishes live
And the dolphins play,
I am looking for the treasure,
The submarine floats so far away,
Ooh look, there's the treasure,
Hip hip hooray.

Grant Munday (9)
Sandford School

AMY

When she's angry she's a raging storm.
When she's pleasant she's the sweetest nectar.
When she's jokey she's the most comical clown.
When she smiles she's a charming princess.
When she's soppy she's a whimpering puppy.
When she cries she's a sea of tears.
When she runs she's the northern wind.
When she shouts she's a roaring lion.
When she draws she's a junior artist.
When she jumps she's a hoppy kangaroo.
When she grins she's a cheeky monkey.
When she climbs she's a clawing leopard.
When she's cold she's Amy Frost.
Yet best, she's my friend Amy.

Sarah Waterworth (9)
Sandford School

A SUNFLOWER FIELD

A blurry field of yellows and browns
And small part of green.
A sunflower is double the size of me.
Beautiful green stem and leaves.
Bright yellow petals as bright as the sun.
Brown centre as brown as the ground
And it is hard to believe
That it all comes from a seed.
That's why it's a hidden treasure to me.

Emma Glass (9)
Sandford School

My Books

I love books, they're so cool,
They make me think of a swimming pool,
My books are very groovy,
That makes me see the movies,
So please help me,
Else I won't get my jewellery.

I love books, they're so real,
They make me think of my old seal,
My books are so crazy,
That makes me all lazy,
So please help me,
Else I won't gain my money.

I love books, they're so good,
They make me think of my neighbourhood,
My books are so handy,
That reminds me of Mandy,
So please help me,
Else I won't get my teddies.

Helena Peters (8)
Sandford School

The Wind And Rain

The wind howls noisily
as it sails along outside.

Meanwhile the rain crashes to the ground,
then in a second thunder starts.

The wind dies off
the storm's over.

Michael Thierens (9)
Sandford School

Hidden Treasures

Today I hid my treasure
in a big hole dark and deep,
coins and gold and all things old
were buried for someone to seek.

Perhaps one day in years to come
my treasure will be found
but my gold and jewels and all things old
are dug deep in the ground.

When I go and dig the garden
I must be careful with the spade
the cross I've marked up on my map
shows where my treasure's laid.

And so my friends I hope in time
my treasure is dug up
and my coins and gold and all things old
will bring someone good luck!

Leigh Kinch (8)
Sandford School

When I Was A Baby

When I was a baby, I was very loud
And sometimes I smelt.
My mum called me an angel.
My dad called me a star.
He said I gleamed when I smiled.
My brother said I was a crybaby,
But I said to myself,
Why?

Miça-Joy Evans (8)
Sandford School

The Treasure Box

Hidden among the weeds
Where no one can see
All encrusted with jewels
Filled with all the treasure in the world
So many different colours it made my eyes twirl
Your hands go numb
Your feet stand still at the bottom of the ocean
I could be a millionaire, but no not I,
I like what I've got,
My sister would cry with delight, boo hoo!
My brother would take it all!
But no, not I, I'll tell you what,
I'll take half and leave the rest for you!

Maia Ruscombe-King (8)
Sandford School

My World

The clouds are green, the water is yellow
The hedges are shaped like marshmallows
The bluebells are red, the tulips are blue
The cows go 'baa' and the sheep go 'moo'
Over the hills not so far away
Is a beach where me and my friends play
On this beach there's an ice cream man
He drives around in a multicoloured van
He sells chocolate candy and sweets to chew
But in my world this food is good for you.

Jessica Sings (9)
South Brent Primary School

COLOURS

What is grey? A cloud is grey
On a very rainy day.

What is green? A plant is green
Carrying a runner bean.

What is black? A pig is black
Eating from the pig food sack.

What is brown? A monkey is brown
In the circus with a clown.

What is white? An owl is white
Flying past the moon so bright.

What is red? A rose is red
Growing in the garden bed.

What is blue? The sea is blue
Carrying fish all the way through.

What is yellow? A desert is yellow
With a camel that gives a bellow.

Jack Warne (9)
South Brent Primary School

AUTUMN

A utumn leaves are falling and blowing all around,
U pside down and crinkled all around,
T rees swinging from side to side, becoming the deadly doom,
U nder all the mud, lives the small gentle creatures,
M y shiny conker collection and horse chestnut shell,
N othing is better than . . . *autumn!*

Jemma Cleave (8)
South Brent Primary School

The Seaside

Smelly seaweed under your feet,
Children swimming in the sea,
Crashing waves, the water salty,
Children building sandcastles,
Sniffing wet dogs, looking for food,
Children eating sandwiches,
Seagulls stealing and squawking,
Children laughing and giggling,
Arking seals in the water,
Children picking pretty shells,
Cockle, scallop, limpet and mussels,
Children with fishing nets,
Prawns, shrimps, crabs and starfish,
Children having lots of fun!

Madeleine Carter (8)
South Brent Primary School

What Is?

What is green? Green is midsummer's grass
Where the people can pass.

What is blue? Blue is a waterfall that splashes
When the water comes down.

What is orange? The sun is orange sparkling in the sky
Where the birds can fly.

What is dark green? The Statue of Liberty's dark green
Which is very keen.

What is every colour?
The rainbow is of course as it shines and sparkles.

Daniel Doherty (9)
South Brent Primary School

What Is Red?

What is red?
A cool dude's car riding down the motorway.

What is black?
A beetle's black, crawling round a rock.

What is white?
A white board is white, sparkling clean.

What is blue?
A small blue feather from my bird's wing.

What is brown?
A cardboard box, jam-packed, full to the top.

What is white?
A shooting star is white, falling down night's face.

Ashley Peake (9)
South Brent Primary School

Autumn

Conkers and chestnuts, with spiky green shells
mixed in with multicoloured leaves, red, orange, brown.
Hallowe'en, Guy Fawkes and harvest time are times we celebrate.
Harvest is for the crops we gather and eat,
Hallowe'en for ghosts, witches and wizards
and Guy Fawkes Night for Guy getting caught.
From the golden fields, the blossoming trees
we gather the fruit and harvest the corn
and store food away for the winter.
We make pickles and jams when winter is nearly here.

Laurie Budden (8)
South Brent Primary School

The Baby

So there I was sitting there,
Feeling his head and his soft brown hair.
He was sucking his thumb with a warm blanket,
Out of his eye I saw a little drip.

I felt a little wriggle from his toes,
And felt soft skin off the top of his nose.
I settled down into the sofa,
And whispered in his ear, 'Err.'

He was only two years old,
So Mum said, 'Don't let him get cold.'
So I tucked him under my blanket.

He was so warm, he began to creep,
So I dozed off and fell fast asleep.
I was only four and my mum came in,
She said, 'How sweet.'

Bea Chapman (8)
South Brent Primary School

Seaside

S melly seaweed carries the tiny plankton
E nergetic fish dart through the water
A rk go the pesky seagulls
S mash go the waves on the rocks in a storm
I n the rockpool hide beadlet anemones
D olphins dive in and out of the waves
E els swim gently though the water.

Michael Harris (8)
South Brent Primary School

The Rainbow

What is red? My tray is red,
I keep my book bag in there.

What is orange? An orange is orange,
It is one of my favourite fruits.

What is yellow? My school book is yellow,
I do lots of work in there.

What is blue? My school shirt is blue,
My favourite colour is blue.

What is indigo? A pen is indigo,
For marking my work.

What is violet? Some cardigans are violet,
Mrs Winhall has a violet cardigan.

Joe Fitzsimmons (9)
South Brent Primary School

Autumn

A utumn is fun, full of conkers and apples
U p a tree, birds' nests, down below, crunchy leaves
T o us autumn is fun, everything is covered with brown, yellow leaves
U nder the grey-blue sky, life is busy and exciting,
creatures wild and free, dance for you with hops and bounds.
M yself, I'm kept busy, collecting wood and leaves for the bonfires.
N obody can be sad in autumn!

Amy Wakeham (9)
South Brent Primary School

The Beauty Of Autumn

I like the season of autumn,
Harvest, conkers, trees,
Drifting leaves,
Orange, red, green,
The list goes on,
Some colours I cannot describe,
Hallowe'en with spooks and ghouls
After that, the next day,
All Saints Day comes around,
Autumn winds, whipping in my face,
Bonfire Night with fireworks,
And the traditional rhyme;
'Remember, remember
The fifth of November,
Gunpowder, treason and plot'.
Some fireworks and rockets,
Others, colourful fountains,
While children play with fizzing sparklers.
Blackberries, raspberries,
Chestnuts dropping down,
Roast them on the fire,
Yum! Yum! Yum!

Alec Gower (8)
South Brent Primary School

Swan Lake

As the swan's graceful body glides around the lake
Like a cloud, white and pure,
Soft, sweet and beautiful in every single way
Cygnets swimming soft and sweet
Like a flower as pretty as can be.

Anna Hylands (8)
South Brent Primary School

Fantasy

Far away in Fantasyland live funny creatures,
Some with blue horns and other strange features,
With weird names like Glabbersnitch,
And one green guy called Ninititch.
The planet is covered in bright red leaves,
Shaken down from gongo trees.
Now these trees are magic things,
When they scream, they make your ears ring.
For transport they use flying crocs,
Who wear fluorescent yellow socks.
All the things in the city only eat one food,
When you eat this special thing you're always in a good mood.
Now to leave this place of trouble,
I say goodbye to you in a space bubble.

Samuel Rowe (9) & Alexander Thomas (10)
South Brent Primary School

Autumn

Autumn days drifting away,
tumbling leaves blowing away.
Coloured leaves, bare stripped trees.
Bonfire night, fireworks fly.
Big red sun floating by,
getting colder every hour.
Autumn going, winter coming,
time flies, say goodbye!

Rosie Fullagar (10)
South Brent Primary School

My Pet Snake

My pet snake is
a wriggly one.
He likes his food
to fill his tum.
His name is Bob,
he slithers in the pond.
He bites the postmen
as they come.

My pet snake has
the name of Bob.
His food is mice,
the stuff that's nice
for snakes, especially
my pet snake!

Matthew Hard (10)
South Brent Primary School

The Baby

When I asked Mum to hold our baby,
She said, 'After Olly.'
So when it was my turn,
Mum gave me our baby.
His skin felt very soft.
He made me feel happy.
Holding him was nice,
Then it was time
To give him back to Mummy.

Robbie Thomas (8)
South Brent Primary School

THE CAT

The cat purrs and sleeps on my lap,
I give it food,
I look after my cat,
I brush,
I clean it,
I look after my cat,
It sleeps on my bed
And that's what makes a cat.
It plays with its toys with hope and joy
And that's what makes my
Cat!

Laura Hannaford (8)
South Brent Primary School

THE BARN OWL

The barn owl is in the barn, starving
We need to feed it,
We need to feed it,
Where has it gone?
It is like a cloud coming towards me
It is like a cloud,
It is like a cloud, like a cloud.
Where has it gone?
Where has it gone?
Where has it gone?

Sian Phillips (9)
South Brent Primary School

The Sea Horse

The ocean lies its way to an open world and sets the sea horse
High upon its legs.
He spits the waves upon their feet,
He spits the waves alive,
We say he goes to meet the calm, lonely seas
Where the sea horse gallops on the waters deep.
We cheer her down and say 'Here, here comes the sea.'

Rowena May Clark (8)
South Brent Primary School

The Lake

The lake is calm and still,
It's always been like that.
It's home to many creatures,
Like swans, fish and plants.
I like it there because it's quiet and peaceful,
The lake is calm and still,
It's always been like that.

Molly Wakeley (9)
South Brent Primary School

Starlight Pony

My starlight pony will do anything for me
She'll canter, trot in a beautiful way
Especially in May,
Because it's bright, hot and sunny.
My parents have lots of money,
That's why I have a starlight pony.

Sophia Skinner (8)
South Brent Primary School

The Waves

The waves are lapping at the beach
Just out of your human reach,
Far out at sea we hear them roar
Deep, deep down on the sea floor.
The waves are flying and jumping,
They are a bit mad, all lumping and bumping.
The waves are lapping at the beach,
The waves are lapping at the beach.

Bridie May Kennerley (7)
South Brent Primary School

The PlayStation

You start playing then
You get sucked in!
We have a battle,
Then we have a drink,
Then we battle again.
I win!

Edward Howard (9)
South Brent Primary School

The Horse

The horse gallops through ocean and seas,
galloping, galloping through the seas.
Come to me,
come little horse,
come to me, come.

Jessica Warren (8)
South Brent Primary School

Puppies

Puppies play together outside,
In the night they woof and howl.

They chew bones,
They don't like being alone.

By the fire it's comfortable, warm and dry,
When every good little puppy sleeps in the night.

In the night puppies will go to bed,
And you'll always want to keep your little puppy,
You'll never want it dead.

Megan Jane Theobald Jones (8)
South Brent Primary School

What Is Green?

What is green? A Christmas tree is green
in the corner of the room.

What is blue? The sea is blue
with the giant waves crashing against the rocks.

What is red? A tomato
juicy and wet with water on it.

What is silver? The moon is silver
beaming on the Earth.

Struan Robertson (9)
South Brent Primary School

COURAGE

Courage is golden,
It smells like daffodils.
Courage tastes like a strong cup of coffee,
It sounds like lions growling,
It feels like a turtle's shell.
Courage lives in your heart.

Roberta Morgan (9)
South Brent Primary School

WAR POEM

War is bloody red,
It smells like gunpowder burning.
War tastes bitter and sour,
It is sharp and jagged,
It sounds screechy and loud.
War lives in a dead, barren wasteland.

Callum Stewart (9)
South Brent Primary School

THE HORSE GALLOPS

Through the field the graceful horse glides,
Water drops falling off the leaves,
Then it goes through the wondrous world,
With a stream and with a mighty *'Splash!'*
It's gone forever and eternity.

Hannah Musgrave (8)
South Brent Primary School

Up In The Attic

(And something's creeping)
clogged up gas mask,
dirty antlers in the corner,
toy combat plane, green,
big ripped British flag,
dusty black top hat,
old heavy lantern,
bright torches,
box of worn out lights,
dusty broken games,
old stuffed badger,
quick snappy mousetrap,
up in the attic.

James Purdy (10)
South Brent Primary School

The Swan

Swan, swan swimming slow,
With your long white wings so low,
With your cygnets following behind,
I know if I come close you'll mind.
Your long white neck is tucked in tight,
With the lake so calm in bright moonlight,
You're so beautiful I'm not letting you go, no, no.
Swan, swan, swimming slow,
Swimming slow,
Swimming slow.

Corinna Paine (9)
South Brent Primary School

The Sea Horse Dance

Sea horse, sea horse, dance with me,
through the sea we twirl and turn.
Through the creatures, through them we sway.
Sea horse, sea horse, come with me
through the ocean, you will see a
beautiful carriage waiting just for you,
making your dreams come true.

Nicole Passmore (9)
South Brent Primary School

Peace

Peace is like white softness,
It smells of lavender perfume,
Peace tastes like creamy cream,
It sounds like birds singing in the sky,
It feels like light blue delicate silk,
Peace is all around us.

Katie Scott (10)
South Brent Primary School

Pleasure

Pleasure is the darkest pink,
It smells of fresh lavender,
Pleasure tastes of assorted chocolates,
It sounds like laughter,
It feels like silk,
Pleasure lives in Heaven.

Charlotte Fisher (10)
South Brent Primary School

HOLE PIPE

I am a hole pipe
People on skates and skateboards
Go round and round and round.
They must get dizzy,
The number of times
They go round and round
They wear me out.

David Partridge (10)
South Brent Primary School

DEATH

Death is jet-black,
It smells like blood, burning blood,
Death tastes of bitterness,
It sounds like an ear-piercing scream,
It feels like the smoothest of silk,
Death lives in Hell!

Martin Briggs (9)
South Brent Primary School

BEING A CHRISTMAS TREE

I am a Christmas tree and I can see,
the presents lying under me.
People crowd round me on Christmas Day,
there they are, they're ready to play.
They've finished now and my star has fallen off.
See!

Jasmin Skinner (9)
South Brent Primary School

UP IN THE ATTIC

(. . . and . . . something's . . . crawling . . .)
Something said *'Boo . . .'*
in the dark, in the shadows
and earphones too.
Morse code machine,
hovering, darting bats,
last year's Christmas lights,
pitch black top hat,
tattered, ripped old game,
clogged up spooky gas mask,
dusty small toy aeroplane,
old cased stuffed dead badgers,
Up in the attic . . .

Tom Nathan Shotter (9)
South Brent Primary School

AT SCHOOL

At school there are teachers, they are really nice
You get to do nice work
You see nice people
You go to an assembly
They have nice equipment
We do games
We do PE
Get nice food
Get nice dinner ladies.

Thomas Salem (8)
South Brent Primary School

COLOURS

What is yellow? The sun is yellow
going down to bed.

What is green? The trees are green
high up in the sky so high.

What is red? A rose is red
standing in the grass.

What is grey? The sky is grey
on a cloudy day.

What is blue? The pond is blue
swaying side to side.

What is purple? The sky is purple
when the sun sets down.

What is pink? A flower is pink
spreading round the garden.

What is white? The moon is white
in the sky so bright.

What is orange? The fish is orange
paddling round the pond.

What is gold? The sun is gold
when the sun rises again.

Amy Passmore (10)
South Brent Primary School

THE SUN IS SWIRLING

The sun is swirling in the sky like honey in the jar,
Splashing on all the cars,
Going far like a twinkling star,
Like a diamond in the sky,
Like someone crying through the sky,
Like some clouds in the sky,
Like a bird in the sky,
Like a sun in the sky.

Rebecca Jones (9)
South Brent Primary School

DOWN AT THE FAIRGROUND

Down at the fairground
I wait, I wait,
I wait for my brother to get off the ride.
I wait, I wait,
I wait in the queue for candyfloss and sweets.
I wait, I wait,
I wait for the ride to end.
I wait, I wait.

Iain Tinkler (8)
South Brent Primary School

THE LION

It makes its pride by roaring loud,
that's what makes his parents proud,
He walks down to the waterhole,
Everybody says hello.

He has a little drink of water,
Then he sees his friend's own daughter.
He feels jealous so he goes to fight her
And nearly kills her.

Nicole Hill (8)
South Brent Primary School

CATS

C ats sleep anywhere
A ny bedroom, any lair,
T iny teddies, little flowerpot,
S leeping in front of a fire so hot.

B eady eyes shut and still
E nding up asleep on a hill
D reamy, sleepy, he floats away,
S leeping heavily all day.

Rebecca Joint (9)
South Brent Primary School

ANIMALS

Snakes are long,
Bears are strong,
Kangaroos jump,
Camels have a hump,
Hedgehogs walk along the lane,
Spiders go down the drain,
Koalas climb up the trees,
Birds fly up in the breeze.

Zoë Pilkington-Rowan (9)
South Brent Primary School

Colours

Colours, red, blue, yellow, green,
White, pink, violet, cream,.
Colours, colours, every day,
the more you see, the more you say.
I love colours, brown, grey, black, more,
even the ones I do not know.
I love colours of every type,
even the silver on the blade of a knife,
even the brown rust on an ancient drainpipe.
I love colours, brown, grey, black, mauve,
even the ones I do not know.

Helena Seager (9)
South Brent Primary School

Chocolate Muffins

Chocolate muffins are like big treats,
They're scrummy and yummy and so good to eat.
I creep through the kitchen throughout the night,
And what do I see right in my sight?
I see a muffin all creamy and brown.
I take it upstairs without a frown
While my dad is drinking his tea,
Mum says, 'Who ate that muffin?'
I say, 'It was me!'

Holly Senior (9)
South Brent Primary School

Light

Light is good, it shows us the way,
Helps us recognise things, it shines all day.
It helps us see things the way they are,
It helps us play from dawn till dark.

Jesus, the light of the world.

Jenny Haley (10)
South Brent Primary School

Hidden

No one understands me,
No one can see,
What I am going through
To be like me.

You would never forgive me,
You'd give me no chance,
You'd look away without one glance.

Seeing me scares you
Like never before,
You don't understand
What I've been through before.

I like to laugh,
To sing and play,
Smiling faces take my cares away.

But you'll never see me,
As I am handicapped,
Feeble and weak,
Left out in the cold and the bleak.

Lucy Harrison (11)
The Maynard School

The Dragon's Cave

Inside a mountain far away,
Which I have not seen until today,
Lies a secret dragon's cave,
Where no man goes - not even the brave,
If you go, that's if you dare,
Be sure - be certain you take good care,
For one man went and never returned,
With the dragon's flames he'd been burnt,
Find the chamber full of gold,
You never will unless you're bold,
The treasure is of the finest sort,
Tread quietly or you will be caught,
The dragon's coat is a fiery red,
If you annoy him you will end up dead,
The dragon is hungry as a rule,
So go back home and don't be a fool.

Alice Woolley (11)
The Maynard School

The Pancake

Up goes the pancake,
Flying through the air,
The scrumptious taste flowing into my stomach,
You just can't get enough.
The creaminess,
The floppiness,
The wonderful tastebuds that belong to me.
That's the hidden treasure.
All the lovely yummy mixture,
Stirring in the bowl,
I hope it will be ready soon,
Because my tummy's rumbling.

Laura Parry (10)
The Maynard School

My Hidden Treasures

I will hide in my box
Photos of family and friends
TJ my teddy bear
My favourite book.

I will stow away in my box
Sea churned blue grass
A drawing of my cat Gabby
A piece of Chinese cane.

I will conceal in my box
The lovely smell of my mum's cooking
The cuddles from Dad
My childhood memories.

I will hide my hidden treasures *forever!*

Felicity Woodgate (10)
The Maynard School

Colour Control

Pink, red, yellow and green,
Tell me paintbrush what have you seen?
'Pens, pencils, pastels and chalk,
And crayons that only talk, talk, talk.

The stencils normally walk away
And come again another day.
The stampers jump about
And make a terrible mess
Until the ink is really considerably less.

That's what happens when the children go out,
And that is why I am now going to *shout!'*

Alison Champernowne (10)
The Maynard School

THE HORSE RACE

The gates are wide open, I kick Swallow on,
I look for the others, they've already gone,
Swallow goes to a gallop and then starts to race,
All the mud and the water sprays up to my face.

We come to the first jump, Swallow soars up and up,
For jumping my Swallow should get a huge cup,
We're going so fast now, Swallow still keeps his pace,
And the second jump we cleared with remarkable grace.

Going faster we overtook all ponies but one,
And this handsome young pony really can run,
We galloped so slow we galloped so fast,
She was always ahead and I always was last.

The next jump we cleared with inches to spare,
I hoped the other would fall but she was still there,
The dapple behind me was coming up quick,
And I wished that my Swallow would give him a kick.

The next jump I cleared and I cleared it alright,
But the dapple wasn't lucky, turned round and took flight,
I was now in the second place and doing quite well,
And the piebald behind me tripped up and fell.

I looked further on, there was miles to go,
And my wonderful Swallow was going quite slow,
Then the rest of the ponies actually caught up,
It didn't look like we're in line for the cup.

Then they all overtook me with a burst of speed,
The very thing I at this moment need,
I was lagging behind and just cleared a jump,
Though it did hurt my bottom since he gave me a bump.

And now in my eyes I catch a glimpse of the end,
If only my Swallow's fastness would mend,
And in a burst of speed at a flash of some light,
Swallow went and won and set things right.

Aoife Quigly (10)
The Maynard School

JADE

Jade was no ordinary girl,
She was different from the rest,
Some people thought that she was bad,
And that she certainly wasn't the best.

Jade was polite and Jade was good,
Jade was very kind,
Jade liked chocolate and a few sweets,
And she had fizzy drinks in mind.

As you know, Jade is green,
A very lovely shade,
But once it is used a lot,
It will begin to fade.

Only one person liked her,
Her name was Marzipan Moo,
She was the only one nice to Jade,
If you were her, would you?

In this twenty lined poem,
Something hasn't occurred,
Jade is someone very special,
Disabled is the word.

Olivia Russell (11)
The Maynard School

HIDDEN TREASURE

One day I found some treasure in a nest
The bird inside was quiet as he was at rest
He was a robin and he had a white vest
The treasure that I found was a blue and pink crest

Because it was blue and pink
It made me think

Where had it come from?
Maybe a bird called Tom
Brought it here from where he used to belong
Which was probably called Ping-Pong, Ding-Dong

One summer's morning
When the sun was just dawning
I found some treasure in a nest

The treasure was pink
And it made me think
Where on earth had it come from.

Fern Varker (10)
The Maynard School

WINTER

Time is ticking,
The sun is sinking,
The world is a dreary grey.
All around me,
Up and down me,
The need to feel a summer's day,
Dawn is arriving,

I am striving,
To keep the winter away.
The light is dimming,
The world is singing,
Winter is here to stay.
Now I shall go back into my house,
It is dreadfully hard being a mouse.

Violet Hunton (11)
The Maynard School

Hidden Treasures

The world has turned its back on me,
Disgust and wariness is all I see,
My face is just a mask of pain,
On which this terrible disease was lain.

No one worries about my destiny,
For I am in the power of leprosy,
I feel weak and lonely and wish someone would care,
But all people do is whisper and stare.

I am on my own in a ruthless place,
And my fearful fate scars my face,
I live in a world of time not told,
And through being scared I will never be bold.

Why would anyone want to be friends with me?
For blisters and rashes are all they can see,
And nobody has ever tried,
To find my hidden treasure inside.

Libby Dixon (11)
The Maynard School

AUTUMN

The crispy leaves on the trees,
golden, brown, red and yellow leaves.
The bark looks old and feels secure,
if it could talk it would be wise and mature.
All trees are very strange,
they have got a hobbit-like range.
You might see a gardener raking the lawn,
looking tired and forlorn.
Everything has an edge,
look something's rustling in the hedge,
don't worry, it's our hedgehog friend,
who thinks the cold months have no end.
It's now six o'clock and already pitch dark,
not many people in the park.
Now I'm tucked up in my bed,
with my teddy by my head.
I've found a hidden treasure in autumn.

Imogen Clifton (11)
The Maynard School

THE FURRY COMFORTER

When the day is stressful,
And my heart is full of cares,
It's nice to know that back at home,
Are all my teddy bears.
As I stumble through the doorway
And fall into a chair,
I know that sitting next to me,
There'll always be a bear.
When no one's sympathetic,

And I feel close to tears,
I always get attention
From those lovely furry ears.
I love them all so dearly,
And though things may go wrong,
When my lovely hug surrounds me,
I don't stay sad for long.

Olivia Matthews (10)
The Maynard School

My Cat Poppy

My pussy cat is a great fat slob
Who sleeps all day.
She gets up for her milk and food
But hardly ever goes out to play.
She is four years old, but looks fourteen
And she doesn't catch mice any longer.
When she does go out
She looks around with absolute wonder.

But I don't care if she is fat
And sleeps all day.
Because she's such a dear old cat
She's my sunny ray.
When she's in my arms she looks at me
With loving dim eyes
And many people say she needs to get thinner.
Poppy, you're the best cat in the world
And oh, please don't get any slimmer.

Annabel Hope (10)
The Maynard School

The Field

The field is so empty,
So big and so bare.
Nothing's inside it and nobody's there.

No farmhouse is near
And the dong, dong, dong,
Of the old grandfather clock has suddenly gone.

But when I turn around
The old cracked wall is still there,
It's been with me all the time,
Or has it never been there . . .

There used to be a tree
And also there a well,
But all is now gone like a ding of an old rare bell.

But suddenly there is a big bright beam
And now I only realise there was no need to be frightened,
It was only a dream.

Elizabeth Stuart (11)
The Maynard School

Quietness

Behind the lonely mountain lies
what seems like an endless plain.
It is deserted - or it seems so . . .
until you find a little lane.

This little land goes on and on,
never stopping . . .
until it narrows right down to a tiny crack
and then opens out to a massive hill.

This massive hill goes up and up,
never stopping . . .
until it opens right out to a plain again,
then all is quiet, all is still.

Sarah Tresidder (11)
The Maynard School

The Woods

Woods are so tender,
The treetops so green,
Greener and greener
Than you've ever seen.

The dewdrops turn to crystal,
And there's a layer of thick, soft moss,
But for all these wondrous things
There must be a boss.

Maybe it's a ghost
Who lives in the brown, harsh bark,
Or maybe it's a demon
Who lives in the dark.

Maybe it's a person
Who lives in the light blue sky,
Or maybe it's a something
Which makes the wind whistle by.

But in a way
It's sad we don't know,
Because it could be a friend,
Or the wood's worst foe.

Rebecca Tilke (10)
The Maynard School

HIDDEN TREASURE

I found a pot of hidden treasure
Buried deep in the sand
It was covered with mud
And when I dropped it with a thud
The ground began to shake

The mud fell off it
But it was chained to a rock
I wish I could get the lid off
But dust flew in my face and I started to cough
And my ship had floated away

It had floated away
I was left by myself
I really wanted to go home
I knew my tummy would start to groan
And my mum would be really worried

I hope I can see her soon.

Lily Black (10)
The Maynard School

ORANGE

Orange is the colour of a tangerine,
Juicy and yummy.
It gives off the feeling of heat,
It is the sun,
Shining down on everyone,
Showering the sky with rays.
Orange is the colour of the sun setting in the sky.
Orange is rich,
Orange is a colour.

Hannah Coates (10)
The Maynard School

Everyone Has A Hidden Treasure Inside

There's no one to love me,
No one to care,
No one to think I'm great.
There's no one to hold me tight at night,
And tell me that everything would be all right.

They laugh at me,
Call me names at play,
They pinch me and punch me,
I feel hated in a way.
But my mum always said,
She said, said she,
That there's a treasure hiding in me.

Nicki Martin (11)
The Maynard School

Hidden Treasures

Hidden treasures my mother used to say
are the things that are special to you.
The things you love and care for.
Like the sun that shines each and every day.
The stars that speckle and the moon that smiles
and glistens every blue night.
Hidden treasures are the things
that make this lovely world so different.
A baby's giggle when you smile at it.
The last leaf that falls to the ground
ready for winter to come.
Smells of beautiful flowers in the sizzling summer.
Fireworks that sparkle in the night-time.

Anoushka Weber (10)
The Maynard School

My Dog

My dog is called Pip,
She might greet you with a nip!
But otherwise she's great,
And she never tries to escape.

But you should see the size of her teeth,
But they wouldn't hurt a thief.
She might seem slightly fat,
It doesn't mean she won't chase a cat.

She goes mad if you throw a tennis ball,
And always comes back when you call.
When she eats her dinner,
She gets fatter, not thinner.

Just when she falls asleep,
The tumble-dryer wakes her with a beep.

But I don't mind if she's fat or thin,
In a race she's bound to win.

She has just become a mum,
And given me another ball of fun.

There's just one thing about my dog,
Which makes my life a bit of a slog.
She sometimes chases my neighbours fowls,
The chickens then squawk and my naughty dog growls.

Katharine Merrick (10)
The Maynard School

My Room

My room is a most wonderful thing,
All covered over in pink.
I never would want a different room,
Now I've got my own.

But yesterday Mum and Dad
Both had some terrible news.
'We are moving house!' Wasn't that bad!
What about my room?

So I asked them,
'When are we going?'
They replied, 'Tomorrow at noon,
But maybe today if you want.'

I hastily said, 'No, tomorrow is fine.'
Then I ran upstairs to my room,
I packed all my stuff, I was missing it already,
So I tore a bit off the wallpaper.

My parents changed their minds,
So we had to go today,
I ran upstairs, as quickly as I could,
And said goodbye to my room.

My new room is an even more wonderful thing,
All covered over in blue.
I never would want a different room
Now that I've got my own.

Maddie Samuels (10)
The Maynard School

My Garden

In my garden, squirrels play,
Butterflies fly and foxes hunt
The flowerbeds are blooming
The trees are growing tall
As they sway, rustling in the wind
And rabbits are feeding their babies so small.
The grass is green
The flowers are blossoming,
The colour coming alive
The leaves are getting greener
And glisten in the sun.
Day by day,
My garden grows.
The birds are singing,
So sweet and beautiful
And building their nests
Ready for their young
The deer roam the garden beds,
In search of something to eat.
Mice scatter quickly along the grass
The sun shining, sparkling in the sky
Dogs barking, yapping when they run
The sound of other children having fun
Bees fly above
In search of nectar
Cats run free
Sniffing out food
The sound of the stream,
Rattling against the rocks
Makes me feel calm inside.

Lucy Quicke (11)
The Maynard School

HIDDEN TREASURES

They laugh at Jessie because she is blind,
And because she reads in Braille, she's behind,
I used to be one of those,
Who laughed at her sight, her shoes and her clothes
But then one day I saw her walk down the road,
With an old lady who helped Jess, to her abode,
The old lady did not laugh or jeer,
She simply said, 'You're home now dear,'
I wondered why the old lady was being kind,
Why should she care if Jess was blind?
I knocked on the door of Jess's home,
A woman answered and said Jess was upstairs, in a kindly tone,
In Jess' room I was lost for words,
I stared out of the window and watched the birds,
I realised that she could not see the birds,
All it was, was their sounds she heard,
So I asked her what she enjoyed at school,
She replied, swimming in the deep, dazzling blue pool,
How do you know that the pool is blue?
Because people who see describe things to me,
People like you,
I said, 'I'll tell you of a pig and you can draw one,
It will be fun,
A pig has a little curly tail and a round pink snout,
It's got four legs, it's pink and it's rather stout,'
She drew the pig, pretty and kind,
And she's going to be my best friend though she's blind,
We're going skating together and over the ice we'll glide,
Because I've found the hidden treasure she holds inside.

Lauren Theaker (11)
The Maynard School

MY SECRET GARDEN

I have a secret garden,
Most people say, 'I beg your pardon.'
When I tell them it can only be seen at midnight,
Where all that can be seen is a flicker of light.
Follow me through secret twists and turns,
And there, well hidden behind thick ferns,
Is a mud coloured puppy who waits for me.
A tree which towers above the rest,
Is most definitely the very best,
On it hangs an amazing swing,
You could say it was fit for the king of kings.
It takes you to another place,
Where there is no such thing as the human race.
The trees all look like mighty lords,
They'd look even grander if they had swords!
Beyond the summer house lies a pond,
Of which I am extremely fond.
Waddling ducks come out to play,
The moon doth shine as bright as day!
Dipping, diving, golden fish,
I wish I hadn't had fish for supper, oh I wish!
I like to pick up slimy toads,
Quite a lot of them, in fact loads and loads,
Have you ever tasted fruit so ripe?
It's completely delicious, just my type.
My puppy loves his midnight run,
He's my favourite garden chum,
He and I have so much fun,
He scares hedgehogs on the enormous lawn,
Oh dear, I have to go now, it's almost dawn.

Lulu Austin (10)
The Maynard School

WAITING AND WALKING

The wind blows around my hair,
The rain lashes down on my face.
Why couldn't my mum just have remembered to pick me up?
The trees scare me,
Their claw-like branches reaching out for me.
At least the ground was the smooth tarmac of the road,
No cars come along it.

The leaves swirl around me,
Falling damp on my head.
Where is Mum?
She should be driving past.
I need her; I don't even have a torch.
I hate her.
Where is she?
I'm too angry to be scared.

An owl hoots. Jump.
'Where are you, come for me Mum.'
Tears of emotion spill down my face as I shout.
The wind drives hard, I can hardly see.
Only, wait.

Is that a light behind?
Through the rain and wind, two headlights come, closer, closer.
I start laughing, I run towards it.
The car stops, the door opens.
The slim, pretty figure of my mum comes out.
I fall into her arms.
Wet and soaking she cried with me.
'You've walked ten miles in the dark.'
'I know, you never came, you never came.'
'I'm here now, my treasure, I'm here.'

Sarah Sheldon (11)
The Maynard School